VOLUME TWO

Wilhelm Meister's Years of
Apprenticeship

VOLUME TWO

WILHELM MEISTER'S YEARS OF APPRENTICESHIP

Wilhelm Meisters Lehrjahre

Books 4–6

by

Johann Wolfgang von Goethe

Translated by
H. M. Waidson

JOHN CALDER · LONDON
RIVERRUN PRESS · DALLAS

This translation from the German first published
1978 in Great Britain by
John Calder (Publishers) Ltd.,
18 Brewer Street, London W1R 4AS
and in the U.S.A. by
riverrun press Inc.,
4951 Top Line Drive, Dallas 75247, Texas

© This translation John Calder (Publishers) Ltd 1978

ISBN 0 7145 3699 7 Cased

Typeset by the Blackburn Times Press, Northgate, Blackburn
Lancashire BB2 1AB in 10pt Plantin. Printed by M. & A.
Thomson Litho, East Kilbride. Bound by Hunter and Foulis Ltd.,
Edinburgh.

CONTENTS

BOOK FOUR

Chapter One

Laertes was standing thoughtfully by the window and, leaning on his arm, was looking out into the open. Philine came quietly across the assembly room towards him, inclined towards him and made fun of his serious appearance.

'Please don't laugh,' he rejoined; 'it is terrible, the way time passes and everything changes and comes to an end. Just look, it was only a short time ago that there was a fine encampment here; how cheerful the tents looked, how lively things were then, how carefully the whole area was guarded! And now all at once everything has disappeared. Just for a short time the trampled straw and the trenches dug out for cooking purposes will still show some traces; then soon it will all be ploughed over, and the fact that so many thousands of vigorous people have been in this place will only be a memory haunting the minds of a few old folk.'

Philine started singing and led her friend into a dance in the assembly room. 'Since we can't run after time once it has gone by,' she cried, 'let us at least revere her gaily and gracefully as a beautiful goddess while she is moving past us.'

They had scarcely taken a few turns when Madame Melina made her way through the room. Philine was malicious enough to invite her likewise to join in the dance and in this way to remind her of the unshapely figure she had acquired in her pregnancy.

'If only I were not to see any woman with child again!' Philine said behind her back.

'Well, she is expecting,' Laertes said.

'But it suits her so badly. Have you noticed the loose fold in the front of her shortened skirt which always goes on ahead whenever she moves? She has no style or skill in looking at herself the least bit critically and in hiding her condition.'

'Oh, let it go,' Laertes said, 'time will no doubt come to her rescue.'

'All the same it would be nicer if children could be shaken down from treetops,' cried Philine.

The Baron came in and uttered a few friendly words to them in the name of the Count and Countess who had left quite early in the day, and gave them some presents. After that he went to Wilhelm who was busy with Mignon in an adjoining room. The child had shown herself very friendly and obliging, had asked after Wilhelm's parents, brothers and sisters, and relations, and in doing so had recalled him to his duty of giving some news of himself to his own family.

Along with greetings of farewell from the master and mistress of the house, the Baron brought him the assurance that the Count had been very pleased with him, his acting, his poetic labours and his theatrical efforts. As a proof of this regard he produced a purse through whose fine texture the attractive colour of new gold coins shimmered; Wilhelm stepped back and refused to accept the purse.

'Regard this gift as a recompense for your time, as an expression of gratitude for your efforts, not as a reward for your talent,' continued the Baron. 'If this last provides a good name and gains people's appreciation, it is only reasonable that our hard work and effort should at the same time make it possible for us to satisfy our needs, as after all we are not just mind alone. If we were in the city, where everything is to be found, this little sum of money would have been transformed into a watch or ring, or something else; but now I am putting the magician's wand directly into your hands; get yourself a jewel for it, one that will be most dear to you and most useful, and keep it as a reminder of us. At the same time, do treat the purse with respect. The ladies knitted it themselves, and their intention was that the container should give to the content the most acceptable form.'

'Do pardon my embarrassment and my misgivings at accepting this present,' Wilhelm replied. 'It destroys, so to speak, what little I have done and inhibits the free play of a happy memory. Money is a fine thing where something is to be disposed of, and I wouldn't like the memory of me to be completely discarded by your establishment.'

'That is not so', the Baron rejoined; 'but since you yourself have delicate susceptibilities, you will not expect the Count to wish to think of himself as being completely in your debt—a man whose greatest ambition is to be courteous and just. He has not failed to notice what a lot of trouble you have taken and how you have devoted your whole time to his concerns, indeed, he knows that you have not been sparing with your own money in order to hasten certain arrangements. How can I look him in the face again if I can't assure him that his expression of gratitude has given you pleasure?'

'If I were allowed to think only of myself and to follow only my own inclinations,' Wilhelm replied, 'I would obstinately refuse to accept this gift, fine and honourable as it may be, in spite of all the reasons given; but I don't deny that at the very moment that it puts me in one embarrassing situation, the gift rescues me from another embarrassing position, the one in which I have been up to now with regard to my parents and which has caused me considerable quiet grief. I have not been the best of managers either with the money or with the time which I have to account for; however, the Count's generosity makes it possible for me to inform my family confidently about the good fortune to which this strange side-track has led me. I sacrifice the sense of tact, which admonishes us on such occasions like a sensitive conscience, to a higher duty, and in order to be able to confront my father boldly, I stand before you in some confusion.'

'It is strange what curious misgivings people have about accepting money from friends and patrons,' the Baron went on again, 'when they would accept any other gift from them with gratitude and pleasure. Human nature has a number of such like idiosyncrasies which lead to the willing creation and careful cherishing of such scruples.'

'Isn't it the same with all points of honour?' Wilhelm said.

'Oh yes,' the Baron replied, 'and with other prejudices. We are unwilling to weed them out, in case we might perhaps be tearing out valuable plants at the same time. But I am always pleased when certain individuals have a sense of what conventions people can and should override, and I like to think of the story of the witty author who wrote some plays for a court theatre which were received by the monarch with wholehearted approval. "I must give him a handsome reward," the generous prince said; "let inquiries be made as to whether some jewel would please him or whether he would not scorn to accept money." In his humorous way the poet replied to the courtier who had been sent to him: "I am extremely grateful for these gracious sentiments, and as the Emperor takes money from us every day, I don't see why I should be ashamed of taking money from him." '

No sooner had the Baron left the room than Wilhelm eagerly counted the money which he had received so unexpectedly and, as he thought, so undeservedly. It seemed as if the value and dignity of gold, which we do not realize until our later years, made themselves known to him for the first time in an anticipatory way when the handsome, gleaming coins rolled out of the pretty purse. He worked out the account and found that he had just as much in hand, in fact even more, as on the day when Philine had caused him to present her with the first bunch of flowers, particularly as

Melina had promised to repay straight away the advance that had been made to him. He considered his own ability with secret satisfaction, and regarded with some little pride the good fortune that had directed and accompanied him. He now took up the pen with confidence in order to write a letter which should at once put an end to any embarrassment his family might feel and should show his behaviour up to now in the most favourable light. He avoided giving an actual narrative and simply hinted at what had happened to him in significant and mysterious phrases. The healthy circumstances of his finances, the living which he owed to his talents, the patronage of the great, the favour of women, a wide circle of acquaintances, the development of his physical and intellectual potentialities, and hope for the future formed such a strange airy vision that Fata Morgana herself could not have effected a stranger blending.

In this happy state of exaltation he continued, after he had finished the letter, with a long monologue in which he recapitulated the content of his letter and pictured to himself an active and worthwhile future. The example of so many fine soldiers had inspired him, Shakespeare's poetry had opened a new world to him, and from the lips of the beautiful Countess he had breathed in an ineffable fire. All that could not, and should not, remain without effect.

The master of horse came and asked whether they had completed their packing. Unfortunately no one apart from Melina had thought of this. Now they were expected to set off in haste. The Count had promised to arrange for the whole company to be provided with transport for some days' journeying; the horses were ready just at that moment and could not be spared for long. Wilhelm inquired about his trunk; Madame Melina had appropriated it. He asked for his money; Melina had packed it with great care right at the bottom of the trunk. Philine said: 'I've still some room in mine,' took Wilhelm's clothes and told Mignon to bring along the rest afterwards. Wilhelm had to accept this, though not without reluctance.

While they were packing and getting ready, Melina said: 'It's annoying for me that we should be travelling as if we were acrobats and mountebanks; I wish Mignon would wear women's clothes and that the Harpist would quickly go and have his beard off.' Mignon held fast to Wilhelm and said very firmly: 'I am a boy, I don't want to be a girl!' The old man kept silent, and Philine took the opportunity to make some humorous remarks at the expense of a peculiarity of their patron, the Count. 'If the Harpist cuts off his beard,' she said, 'he had better sew it on to tape and keep it carefully so that he can at once take it out as soon as he should happen to meet the Count anywhere in the world; for it was this beard alone which procured him this gentleman's favour.'

When the others took this up with her and demanded an explanation for this strange statement, this is how she put it: 'The Count believes that it contributes a great deal to the illusion if the actor carries on with his part and keeps his character role in his everyday life as well; this is why he favoured the Pedant so much, and it was his opinion that it was quite a good idea that the Harpist wore his false beard not only in the evening on the stage, but also all through the day, and he was very pleased at the natural appearance of the masquerade.'

While the others were making fun of this mistake and of the Count's peculiar opinions, the Harpist took Wilhelm on one side, said goodbye to him and with tears in his eyes requested him to release him at once. Wilhelm spoke encouragingly to him and assured him that he would protect him against anybody, and that nobody would touch a single hair of his, let alone cut it against his will.

The old man was very agitated, and a strange fire glowed in his eyes. 'This is not what is driving me away,' he exclaimed; 'for a long time now I have been quietly reproaching myself for remaining with you. I ought not to linger anywhere, for misfortune hastens upon me and is harmful to those who are associated with me. You have everything to fear, if you do not release me, but don't ask me; I am not my own master, I cannot stay.'

'Who is your master? Who can exercise such force over you?'

'Leave me, sir, with my terrible secret, and let me go. The vengeance that pursues me is not that of an earthly judge; I am the subject of an inexorable fate, I cannot, I may not stay!'

'I certainly shan't let you go in the condition I see you in now.'

'It would be high treason to yourself, my benefactor, if I were to hesitate. With you I am safe, but you are in danger. You don't know who it is you are cherishing at your side. I am guilty, but more unfortunate than guilty. My presence scares away good fortune, and a good deal becomes valueless when I approach. My life should be one of flight and restlessness, to ensure that I should not be overtaken by my unhappy guardian spirit which only pursues me slowly and makes itself noticed when I want to lay down my head and rest. I can't show my gratitude to you in a better way than by leaving you.'

'Strange fellow! It is as difficult for you to take away from me my trust in you as to take away my hope of seeing you happy. I don't wish to intrude into the secrets of your superstition; but if in fact you live with intuitions of wondrous links and premonitions, let me say to you, for your consolation and cheer: "Associate yourself with my happiness, and we will see whose guardian spirit is the stronger, your dark one or my light one!"'

Wilhelm took the opportunity to say much else that was comforting to him; for he had believed for some time now that he could see in his strange companion someone who had burdened himself through chance or destiny with some great guilt and was continually dragging the memory of it around with him. Only a few days earlier Wilhelm had overheard him singing and had taken note of these lines:

> The morning sun glows all aflame
> And lights for him the pure horizon,
> And over his head in its guilt and shame
> The world's whole lovely scene collapses.

The old man could now say whatever he pleased, Wilhelm always had a stronger argument, had a way of interpreting everything in the most favourable way, and was able to talk in such honest, cordial and consolatory terms that the old man himself seemed to become more cheerful again and to be turning away from his melancholy thoughts.

Chapter Two

Melina hoped to find a place with his theatre company in a small but prosperous town. They were already at the locality to which the Count's horses had brought them and were looking around for other coaches and horses with which they hoped to move on further. Melina had taken over the transport arrangements and moreover, as was usual with him, showed himself as very mean. On the other hand Wilhelm had the Countess's fine ducats in his pocket, and believed he had every right to make cheerful use of them; he very easily forgot that he had already mentioned them very boastfully in the imposing statement of account that he had sent to his family.

His friend Shakespeare, whom he acknowledged with great joy as his godfather and for whose sake he was all the more willing to be called Wilhelm, had introduced him to a prince who for a period spent his time in low, indeed bad company, and for all his noble nature took pleasure in the roughness, unseemliness and silliness of such wholly sensuous fellows. The ideal situation with which he could compare his present position was most welcome to him, and self-deception, to which he was almost irresistibly drawn, became much easier for him in this way.

He now began to think about his clothes. He decided that a little waistcoat, over which in case of need a short cloak could be worn, would be very appropriate attire for a traveller. Long knitted trousers and a pair of laced boots seemed to be the true garb of a walker. Then he acquired a beautiful silk sash which he first wrapped round himself with the excuse of needing to keep his body warm; on the other hand he freed his neck from the servitude of a tie and had some strips of calico fixed on to his shirt, though they came out rather wide and looked completely like a collar of the classical period. The beautiful silk neckerchief, the memento of Mariane that he had saved, would lie lightly fastened beneath the calico ruff. A round hat with a bright ribbon and a large feather made the masquerade complete.

The ladies assured him that this outfit suited him extremely well. Philine made herself out as quite enchanted by it and asked to be given his beautiful hair, which he had cut mercilessly in order to approach the more closely to the natural ideal. She made herself quite popular by this approach, and our friend, whose generosity had given him the right to behave like Prince Hal in his manners with the others, soon acquired the taste himself for initiating and encouraging some mad tricks. They fenced and danced, made up all kinds of games, and light-heartedly they enjoyed in strong measure the tolerable wine that was available, and in the disorderliness of this manner of life Philine was lying in wait for our prim hero, and may his guardian spirit take care on his behalf!

A particular pastime which especially entertained the company consisted in extempore pieces of acting in which they initiated and parodied their former patrons and benefactors. Some of them had taken very good note of the external perculiarities of various elevated personages, and the counterfeiting of these latter was received with the greatest applause by the rest of the company, and when Philine brought out from the secret archives of her experiences a few special declarations of love which had been made to her, they could hardly contain themselves for laughing and gloating.

Wilhelm reproached them for their ingratitude; but he was told in reply that they had put in enough work for what they had received there and that in any case the behaviour shown to such meritorious people as they claimed to be had not been of the best. Then they complained about the lack of respect they had received and the way they had been slighted. The mockery, teasing and mimicry started up again, and they became ever more bitter and unjust.

'I could have wished,' Wilhelm said at this point, 'that envy and egotism did not show themselves in what you have been saying, and that you could look at those people and their circumstances from the right point of view. It is a peculiar position to be placed at an elevated level of human society simply through birth. He whom inherited wealth has procured complete ease in life and who finds himself amply surrounded by all the accessories man can desire from his early days onward, if I may put it like this, mostly becomes accustomed to regard these good things as the first and greatest necessities, and he does not see so clearly the value of a personality that has been finely equipped by nature. The behaviour of those of high rank towards lesser people and also to one another is calculated according to external preferences; they will grant to everyone the use of his title, his rank, his clothes and his carriage, only not that of his merits.'

The company applauded these words immoderately. It was found revolting that a man of merit always had to stay in the background and that there were no traces of natural and heartfelt social contact in the world of fashion. This last point in particular gave rise to a lot of detailed discussion.

'Don't blame them for it,' Wilhelm exclaimed, 'be sorry for them, rather. For they seldom have an enhanced awareness of that happiness which we recognize as the highest and which flows from the inner wealth of nature. Only we poor folk, who own little or nothing, have been permitted to enjoy the happiness of friendship in generous measure. We cannot raise our loved ones by grace, nor promote them by favours nor make them happy by presents. We have nothing except ourselves. We must give away this whole self and, if it is to be of any value, the gift should be assured to our friend for ever. What pleasure, what good fortune, both for giver and receiver! What a blissful position loyalty puts us in! It gives a heavenly certainty to the transience of human life; it comprises the main capital basis of our wealth.'

Mignon had approached him while he was saying these words, putting her slender arms around him and standing with her little head leaning on his breast. He placed a hand on the child's head and went on: 'How easy it is for a great personage to gain loyalty! How easy to acquire affection! An agreeable, easy-going and only relatively humane manner can work wonders, and how many ways he has of retaining loyalty once it has been acquired. Everything comes more rarely as far as we are concerned, everything gets more difficult, and how natural it is that we attach a greater value to what we earn and achieve. What touching examples there are of faithful servants who have sacrificed themselves for their masters! How finely Shakespeare has portrayed such figures! In such a case loyalty is the striving of a noble disposition to become like a greater personage. Through constant attachment and love the servant comes to resemble his master, who otherwise is only justified in seeing him as a paid slave. Indeed, these virtues are only for the lower classes; they can't manage without them, and they suit them well. He who can buy himself off easily will equally easily be tempted to dispense with gratitude. Yes, it is in this sense that I believe I can maintain that a great man can have friends, but cannot be a friend.'

Mignon pressed against him ever more closely.

'All right,' someone out of the company replied, 'we don't need their friendship and have never asked for it. Only they ought to know more about the arts, if they do in fact want to protect them. When we were acting at our best, nobody listened to us; it was all a matter of taking sides. If they favoured somebody, he went down well, and they weren't favourable to the person who deserved praise. It was quite improper, how often attention and applause were given to what was silly and tasteless.'

'When I think of the part played by malicious pleasure and irony,' Wilhelm added, 'I can't help thinking things happen in art as they do in life. How is the man of affairs, with his life of busy distractions, to acquire the inward sensitivity in which an artist must remain if he is to produce something that is perfect, and which may not remain unfamiliar to the person who wishes to give the sort of appreciation which the artist hopes for and wishes?

'Believe me, my friends, it is the same with artistic gifts as it is with virtue: they have to be loved for their own sake, or else be given up entirely. And yet neither can be otherwise recognized and rewarded than by being practised in seclusion, like a dangerous secret.'

'And meanwhile, until some connoisseur finds us, we can die of starvation,' someone called out from the corner.

'Not straight away,' Wilhelm rejoined. 'In my experience, so long as a man is alive and bestirs himself, he will always find enough to eat, even if the food is not the richest. And what have you got to complain about? Were we not given a good reception and good hospitality in quite an unexpected way, just when things seemed to be at their worst for us? And now, when as yet we are not short of anything, does it occur to us to do anything to keep in practice and to make further efforts of some kind? We concern ourselves with strange matters and like schoolchildren we banish anything that might remind us of our lessons.'

'It's true,' said Philine, 'it is irresponsible! Let's choose a play; let's act it on the spot. Everyone must do his best, as if he were in front of the largest audience.'

They did not spend long thinking it over; the play was decided on. It was one of those which were much applauded at that time in Germany, and have now been forgotten. Some whistled an overture, everyone thought quickly about his part, they started and went through the play with the greatest care, and really it was good beyond expectations. They applauded each other in turn; it was seldom that things had gone so well.

When they had finished they all sensed an exceptional feeling of satisfaction, partly because of their well-spent time, partly because each could be particularly pleased with himself. Wilhelm praised them extensively, and their conversation was gay and cheerful.

'You should see how far we should get,' our friend cried out, 'if we continued our rehearsals in this way and did not merely limit ourselves with a mechanical sense of duty and craftsmanship to learning by heart, rehearsing and acting. How much more praise musicians earn, how much pleasure they experience, how precise they are, when they tackle their practising together! What efforts they make to keep their instruments in tune, how precisely they keep time, and with what delicacy they can bring out the loudness and the softness of a note! It does not occur to anyone to push himself forward, when someone has a solo, by means of an over-loud accompaniment. Everyone tries to play in the spirit and meaning intended by the composer, and to give good expression to what has been entrusted to him, whether it is much or little. Should we not set about our task with just as much exactness and intelligence, since we are pursuing an art which is a lot more delicate than any kind of music, for it is our calling to describe both the most usual and the strangest utterances of mankind in a tasteful and entertaining manner. Can anything be more detest-able than to be slovenly in rehearsal and to trust to luck during the performance? We should see it as our greatest good fortune and pleasure to be in harmony with one another and to be pleased with each other's performance, and to value the audience's approval only in so far as we had, as it were, already guaranteed it amongst ourselves. Why is the conductor surer of his orchestra than the producer is of his play? Because in an orchestra everyone must be ashamed of his mistakes which offend the ear physically; but how rarely have I seen an actor acknowledge and be ashamed of mistakes, both pardonable and unpardonable, which are so base an offence to the inward ear! I only wish that the stage could be as narrow as the wire of a tightrope-walker, so that no clumsy person would venture up, instead of, as it is now, everyone feeling capable of parading on it.'

The company received this speech kindly, each one being convinced that the words could not be referring to him, since he had recently shown himself so well by the side of the others. It was further agreed that during this tour and in future, if they should stay together, there should be a sociable form of working together, in the spirit of which they had begun. They only thought that since this was a matter of good mood and free choice, there should not in fact be any intervention on the part of a manager. It was taken as settled that among good people the republican constitutional form was the best; it was maintained that the office of manager should go round; he should be elected by everybody and a kind of small senate should be attached to him at all times. They were so enamoured of this thought that they wanted to put it into effect immediately.

'I've no objection,' Melina said, 'if you want to make such an experiment while we are travelling; I will gladly defer my managerial role until we are once more in a settled spot.' He was hoping to save money in this way and push a number of the expenses on to the little republic or on to the interim manager. Now they had a very vigorous discussion as to how they could best arrange the form of the new state.

'It is a mobile kingdom,' Laertes said; 'at least we shan't have any frontier disputes.'

They got down to business at once and elected Wilhelm to be the first manager. The senate was set up, the women were given seats and votes, laws were proposed, there were rejections, there were acceptances. Time passed unnoticed in the course of this game, and because they were spending the time pleasantly, they believed also that they had been doing something really useful and that had opened up a new prospect for the nation's theatre.

Chapter Three

Wilhelm now hoped, as he saw the company to be in such good humour, that he would also be able to discuss with them the literary merit of the plays. 'It is not enough,' he told them, when they came together again the next day, 'for the actor just to look at a play in a perfunctory manner, to judge it according to the first impression it makes and to express his pleasure or displeasure at it without examining it. This is no doubt permissible to a member of the audience who is willing to be moved and entertained, but in fact doesn't want to pass judgment. The actor, on the other hand, ought to be able to give an account of the play and to justify the reasons for his praise and criticism: and how can he do this, if he doesn't know how to penetrate into the meaning and intentions of his author? In the last few days I have noticed so markedly in myself the fault of judging a play from the point of view of one role and of looking at one role only on its own and not in the context of the play, that I would like to recount this example to you, if you will be so good as to give me a hearing.

'You know Shakespeare's incomparable *Hamlet* from a reading which gave you the greatest pleasure some time ago at the castle. We made up our minds to perform the play, and I had taken on the part of the Prince without knowing what I was doing; I thought I was studying it when I started memorizing the strongest passages, the soliloquies and those scenes where power of soul, elevation of mind and vitality have free play, and where a temperament that has been emotionally moved can exhibit itself in expressions of feeling.

'I also thought I was penetrating truly into the spirit of the part if I took upon myself, so to speak, the burden of deep melancholy, and bearing the weight of this pressure, attempted to follow my model through the strange labyrinth of so many moods and eccentricities. So I learnt by heart and rehearsed, and gradually believed that I was becoming identified with my hero.

'Only the further I got, the more difficult it was for me to imagine the whole work, and in the end it seemed to me to be impossible to achieve an overall view. Then I went through the play in an uninterrupted sequence, but here too unfortunately various things didn't fit in for me. Now the characters, now the mood seemed to be inconsistent, and I almost despaired of finding a register in which I could deliver the whole part with all its deviations and shading. For a long time I made vain efforts in these labyrinths, until at last I hoped to be able to approach my goal by a very particular route.

'I sought out every trace that showed itself of Hamlet's character in the early days before his father's death; I noticed what this interesting young man had been independently of this sad event and of the terrible happenings that followed, and what he might perhaps have been without them.

'Delicate and noble in its origin, the royal flower grew forth amidst the direct influences of majesty; the concept of right and of princely dignity, the sense of what was good and decent, along with consciousness of his high birth, developed within him together. He was a prince, a born prince, and wished to rule only so that good people could live a good life without hindrance. Pleasant in appearance, well-bred by nature, sincerely agreeable, he was to be a model for youth and to become a joy to the world.

'Without there being any conspicuous passion, his love for Ophelia was a quiet anticipation of sweet requirements; his eagerness to undertake knightly exercises was not entirely original; on the contrary, this pleasure had to be intensified and enhanced by the praise bestowed upon a third person; with purity of feeling he could pick out honest people and could appreciate the calm which an upright person can experience before a friend's open heart. To a certain degree he had learnt how to discern and appreciate the good and the beautiful in the arts and sciences; anything in bad taste was repugnant to him, and if hatred could flourish in his sensitive temperament, it was only as far as was necessary in order to despise unreliable and disloyal courtiers and to make fun of them in mockery. He was calm in character, simple in conduct, he did not over-relish leisure nor was he all too desirous of occupation. He seemed to be continuing an academic, lounging way of life at court as well. He possessed more cheerfulness as a matter of mood than as heartfelt, he was good company, pliant, modest, attentive, and could forgive and forget an insult; but he could never be at one with somebody who overstepped the limits of what was right, good and decent.

'When we read through the play together again, you can judge whether I am on the right track. At least I hope to be able to back up my interpretation thoroughly with references.'

His description was loudly applauded; people thought they could predict that now Hamlet's behaviour could be clearly explained; they expressed pleasure at this way of penetrating into the writer's mind. Everyone resolved that he too would study some play or other in this manner and explain the author's meaning.

Chapter Four

The company only had to stay at the locality for a few days, but some not displeasing adventures at once began to take shape as far as some members of the group were concerned; Laertes in particular was given encouragement by a lady who had an estate in the neighbourhood, though he behaved towards her extremely coldly, indeed clumsily, and on that account had to put up with much mockery from Philine. She took the opportunity of recounting to our friend the unhappy love-story on account of which the poor young man had become hostile to the whole female sex. 'Who will take it amiss, as far as he is concerned,' she exclaimed, 'that he hates a sex that has treated him so badly and made him swallow down in one gulp all the evils which men may have to fear of women? Just imagine: within twenty-four hours he was lover, fiancé, married man, cuckold, patient and widower! I can't think how things could be made worse for anybody.'

Laertes hurried out of the room, half laughing and in part annoyed, and Philine in her most charming way began to tell the story of how Laertes as a young man of eighteen, just after joining a theatre company, had met a beautiful fourteen-year old girl who was just then intending to depart with her father, who had quarrelled with the manager. He had fallen completely in love at first sight, made all possible representations to persuade the father to stay and had finally promised to wed the girl. After some pleasant hours of being engaged he had married, he had spent a happy night as husband, and then next morning, while he was at rehearsal, his wife had honoured him according to his position with antler adornment; but, Philine went on, because he had hurried home much too early out of excessive fondness, he had unfortunately found an older lover in his place, had set about him with senseless fury, had challenged both lover and father and had come out of the affair with a sizeable wound. After that father and daughter had made off that very night, and he had remained behind, doubly wounded unfortunately. His misfortune had led him to the worst medical man in the world, and the poor fellow had come out of the adventure regrettably with black teeth and running eyes. She felt sorry for him, since furthermore he was the finest fellow walking on God's earth. 'In particular,' she said, 'I am sorry that the poor fool now hates women: for how can anyone who hates women expect to live?'

Melina interrupted them with the news that everything was completely ready for the departure and that they could leave early in the morning. He handed them a schedule about how they were to travel.

'If a good friend will take me on his lap,' Philine said, 'I shall be content about our sitting close together and in a wretched style; anyway, everything's all the same to me.'

'It doesn't matter,' said Laertes, who came along as well.

'It's annoying!' Wilhelm said and hastened away. In return for his money he found a further, quite convenient coach, which Melina had rejected. Another distribution arrangement was made, and people were pleased at the prospect of being able to make their departure in a comfortable manner, when the critical news became known that a volunteer corps had been seen and that not much good was expected to come of this.

In the locality itself people were very much on the alert as a result of this information, even though it was only uncertain and ambiguous. From the position of the armies it seemed impossible that an enemy force could have slipped through, or that a friendly one could have remained so far behind. Everyone was zealous in describing to our company in lurid colours the dangers awaiting them, and in advising them to go by another route.

Most of the actors were plunged into agitation and fear by the situation, and when according to the new republican form all members of the group had been summoned together to confer about this extraordinary position, they were almost unanimously of the opinion that they would have to avoid the danger and stay where they were, or else get out of its way and choose another route.

It was Wilhelm alone, not overcome by fear, who considered it disgraceful to give up at this time a plan, which had been worked out in so much detail, because of a mere rumour. He gave them courage, and his arguments were manly and convincing.

'As yet,' he said, 'it is nothing but a rumour, and how many of these arise in the course of a war! Knowledgeable people say that the possibility is highly unlikely, in fact almost impossible. Ought we to let ourselves be swayed in so important a matter by such uncertain talk? The route which the Count has indicated to us, and for which our travel permit is valid, is the shortest, and it's the one which will be the best way for us. It takes us to the city where there is the prospect of contacts and acquaintances and friends and where you can hope to have a good reception. The détour will also take us there; but what wretched roads it will involve us in, and what distances it will lead us! Can we hope to find our way out of such a situation at this late time of year? And how much time and money will be frittered away in the meantime?' He said still more and presented the matter from so many advantageous angles that their fears lessened and their courage increased. He was able to tell them so much about the discipline of the regular troops and to depict the marauders and vagrants as so worthless, and even to portray danger in pleasant and cheerful terms, that everyone's spirits were raised.

From the very first moment Laertes was on his side, assuring him that he would not be vacillating nor would he give way. The Blustering Old Man found at least a few expressions of agreement in his own way, Philine laughed at them all, and as Madame Melina, who for all her advanced pregnancy had lost none of her natural stout-heartedness, thought the proposal heroic, Melina could not resist, although in any case he hoped to save a lot by taking the nearest route, according to the arrangement that had been made, and so the proposal was accepted with full agreement.

Now they began to take steps for self-defence in case of need. They bought big hunting-knives and hung them in handsomely embroidered slings over their shoulders. In addition, Wilhelm put a pair of small pistols in his belt, while Laertes had a good musket with him as well, and everyone set out on their way with great cheerfulness.

On the second day the drivers, who were no doubt familiar with the district, suggested stopping for the midday break on a wooded upland spot, since the village was far away and people liked to go this way when conditions were good.

The weather was fine, and everybody found it easy to agree to the proposal. Wilhelm took the lead and hurried on foot through the hills, and everyone whom he encountered could not help being taken aback on account of his strange appearance. He hurried up through the woods with quick, contented steps, with Laertes whistling behind him; it was only the women who consented to being transported in the coaches. Mignon likewise went on foot, proud of the hunting-knife which they could not refuse to let her have when the company was being armed. She had wound round her hat the string of pearls which Wilhelm had retained from amongst his mementos of Mariane. Blonde-haired Friedrich was carrying Laertes's musket, and the Harpist had the most peaceable appearance. His long cloak was fixed into his belt, and so he could walk more freely. He had a gnarled staff as support; his harp had been left in one of the coaches.

After they had climbed, not without some difficulty, up to the heights, they at once recognized the open space that had been pointed out to them by the beautiful beech-trees that surrounded and screened it. A large, gently sloping forest meadow was an invitation to linger; an enclosed spring offered the most attractive refreshment, and in between ravines and wooded ridges on the other side a distant, beautiful and promising view could be seen. Villages and mills lay down in the valleys, there were small towns in the plain, and new mountains which were coming into sight in the distance made the panorama even more promising, since they only showed themselves as a gentle restraint.

The first arrivals took possession of the area, relaxed in the shade, started a fire and were making themselves busy and singing as they awaited the rest of the company which came along gradually and with one voice praised the fine weather and the indescribably lovely district.

Chapter Five

If they had often enjoyed good and cheerful hours together between four walls, they were naturally all the more lively here, where the freedom of the heavens and the beauty of the locality appeared to be purifying every heart. They all felt closer to one another, wishing to spend their whole lives in such a pleasant sojourn. They were envious of huntsmen, charcoal-burners and woodcutters, who were kept to these happy places of residence by their calling; above all else, however, they praised the charming way of life of a group of gypsies. They envied the strange fellows who are entitled to enjoy all the adventurous attractions of nature in blissful leisureliness; they were happy to be resembling them to some extent.

In the meantime the women had started to boil potatoes and to unpack and prepare the food they had brought with them. There were some pots by the fire, and the company spread themselves out in groups beneath the trees and among the bushes. Their strange clothes and their varied weapons gave them an unusual appearance. The horses were being fed apart, and if the coaches had been hidden, the sight of this little troop would have been convincingly romantic.

Wilhelm experienced a pleasure that he had never felt before. He could imagine that here was a colony on the move, and that he was its leader. With this in mind he chatted to everyone and developed the illusion of the moment in as poetic a manner as possible. The company's mood became enhanced; they ate, drank and made merry, declaring repeatedly that they had never experienced finer moments.

The merriment had not become more pronounced for long before the urge to activity was aroused in the young people. Wilhelm and Laertes took up their rapiers, and now began their exercising with a theatre purpose in mind. They wanted to enact the duel in which Hamlet and his opponent come to so tragic an end. Both friends were convinced that in this important scene it was not enough to lunge back and forth in a clumsy manner, as no doubt is usually the case on the stage; they were hoping to offer a model as to how a performance could provide a worthy spectacle for fencing experts too. The others formed a circle around them; they both fought with zeal and understanding, and the spectators' interest increased with every pass.

All at once, however, a shot fell in the nearest bush and immediately afterwards a second one, and the company scattered in terror. Soon armed men could be seen making their way to the spot where the horses were having their fodder not far from the laden coaches.

The entire womenfolk emitted a shriek, while our heroes threw away their rapiers, took hold of their pistols, hastened up to the robbers and amidst lively threats called them to account for what they were doing.

After they had been laconically answered with a few musket-shots, Wilhelm fired his pistol at a curly-headed fellow who had climbed into the coach and was cutting the cords around the luggage. The latter, having been truly hit, at once fell down; Laertes too had not missed with his shot, and both friends were drawing their side-arms in good spirit, when a section of the robber-band rushed at them with cursing and shouting, aimed some shots at them and opposed their boldness with gleaming sabres. Our young heroes acted bravely; they called to their other menfolk and encouraged them to set up a general defence. But soon Wilhelm saw no more and lost consciousness of what was going on. Benumbed by a shot which wounded him between the chest and left arm and by a blow which split open his hat and almost penetrated to his brain-pan, he collapsed and was only able to hear about the unhappy end of the raid as a narrative after the event.

When he opened his eyes again, he found himself in the strangest situation. The first thing that confronted him through the mist still before his eyes was Philine's face which was bending over his own. He felt weak, and when he made a movement to lift himself up, he discovered that his head had been on Philine's lap, where it soon sank back again. She was sitting on the grass, had pressed gently to herself the head of the young man lying stretched out before her and had prepared a gentle resting-place for him in her arms, as far as she could. Mignon, with tousled, blood-stained hair, was kneeling at his feet, embracing them amidst many tears.

When Wilhelm saw his bloody clothes, he asked with broken voice where he was, and what had happened to him and the others. Philine begged him to remain quiet; the others, she said, were all safe, and nobody was wounded except himself and Laertes. She was unwilling to tell him anything further and implored him to stay quiet, because his wounds had only been bound poorly and in haste. He stretched out his hand to Mignon and inquired about the reason for the child's blood-smeared hair, believing that she too was wounded.

In order to soothe him, Philine related how this affectionate creature, at seeing her friend injured, had not been able to think on the spur of the moment of any way of staunching the blood; she had used her own hair, loose as it was, to close the wounds, but had soon had to desist from this vain endeavour. Later he had been bound up with sponge and moss, and Philine had also contributed her neckerchief.

Wilhelm noticed that Philine was sitting with her back against her trunk, which still looked quite well locked and undamaged. He asked whether the others had also been lucky enough to rescue their belongings. She answered with a shrug of the shoulders and a glance at the meadow, where broken chests, burst trunks, slit portmanteaux and a mass of small objects lay scattered up and down. There was no one to be seen on the open meadow, and the strange group was alone in this solitude.

Now Wilhelm kept on learning more than he wanted to know: the rest of the men, who might indeed have continued to resist, had been filled with terror right away and had soon been overpowered; some of them took flight, some looked on at the calamity in fright. The drivers, who had held out most stubbornly because of their horses, had been thrown down and tied up, and within a short time everything had been pillaged and dragged off. As soon as their fear for their lives was passed, the anxious travellers began to bemoan their losses, hurried as quickly as they could to the nearest village, taking the slightly wounded Laertes with them, and took away with them only a few remnants of their possessions. The Harpist had leant his damaged instrument up against a tree, and had hastened to the village in order to look for a surgeon and to bring help, if possible, for his benefactor who had been left behind as if dead.

Chapter Six

Our three unfortunate adventurers, however, remained some time longer in their strange plight; nobody came to their help. Evening came, and night threatened to fall; Philine's equanimity started to turn into agitation; Mignon ran up and down, and the child's impatience increased every moment. Finally, when their wish was granted and people were approaching them, they were overcome by a new terror. They could distinctly hear a number of horses approaching by the track which they had come along, and they feared that once more a company of uninvited guests might be visiting this battlefield in order to do some gleaning.

How agreeable was their surprise therefore when a lady on a white horse appeared before their eyes, having come from the bushes; she was accompanied by an oldish gentleman and some horsemen; grooms, servants and a troop of hussars followed.

Philine who opened her eyes widely in surprise at this sight was about to call out and to implore help of the beautiful Amazon, when the latter, already in some surprise, directed her eyes to the strange group, at once turned her horse, rode up and came to a halt. She inquired urgently about the wounded man whose position, in the lap of the frivolous Samaritan, apparently seemed very strange to her.

'Is he your husband?' she asked Philine. 'He is simply a good friend,' the latter replied in a tone of voice which was most displeasing to Wilhelm. He had fixed his gaze upon the gentle, noble, quiet and sympathetic features of the lady who had just arrived; he believed that he never had seen anything more excellent or more charming. A man's overcoat acted as a loose covering and concealed her figure from him; she had borrowed it evidently from one of her companions as protection against the cool evening air.

Meanwhile the horsemen had also come nearer; some dismounted, the lady did so as well, and she inquired with considerate sympathy about all the circumstances of the mishap that had befallen the travellers, especially about the young man's wounds. Then she turned quickly away and went with an old gentleman on one side towards the coaches which came slowly up the hill and halted at the scene of the affray.

After the young lady had been standing a short time by the door of one coach and had been talking to those who had just arrived, a square-built man got out whom she conducted to our wounded hero. He could soon be identified as a surgeon because of the little box that he had in his hand and because of his leather case with its instruments. His manners were rough rather than polite, but his hand was gentle and his help welcome.

He made a thorough investigation, and declared that the wounds were not dangerous, and that he would dress them on the spot, after which the injured man could be taken to the nearest village.

The young lady's worries seemed to become more pronounced. 'Just look,' she said after she had walked up and down a few times and had brought up the old gentleman again. 'Just look at the way he's been treated! And isn't it on our account that he is suffering now?' Wilhelm heard these words and did not understand them. She walked restlessly up and down; it seemed as if she could not tear herself away from the sight of the wounded man, and as if at the same time she was afraid of offending propriety if she stood still at the time when a start was being made, though with some trouble, at undressing him. The surgeon was just cutting up the left sleeve when the old gentleman approached and in a serious tone of voice put before her the urgency of their continuing their journey. Wilhelm had fixed his eyes upon her and had been so captivated by her glances that he scarcely felt what was being done to him.

In the meantime Philine had stood up in order to kiss the lady's hand. When they stood side by side, our friend thought that he had never seen such a contrast. Philine had never before appeared to him in so unfavourable a light. As it seemed to him, she should not come near, let alone touch, that noble creature.

The lady put various questions to Philine, but in a quiet voice. In the end she turned to the old gentleman who was still standing close by in an uninvolved manner, and she said: 'Dear Uncle, may I be generous at your expense?' She thereupon took off the overcoat, and it was evident that her intention was to present it to the unclad, wounded man.

Wilhelm, whose attention had been held up to now by the healing glance of her eyes was now surprised, as the coat was removed, by her beautiful figure. She came closer and placed the coat gently over him. At this moment, when he was intending to open his mouth and stammer a few words of thanks, the vivid impression of her presence had such a strange effect upon his already strained senses that all at once it appeared to him as if her head were encircled by rays and as if a gleaming light were gradually suffusing her whole person. Then the surgeon happened to touch him rather less gently as he set about removing the bullet which was lodged in the wound. The angelic figure disappeared before Wilhelm's eyes as he swooned; he lost consciousness, and when he came to again, the horsemen and the coach together with the beautiful lady and her companions had disappeared.

Chapter Seven

After our friend's wounds had been bound up and he had been dressed again, the surgeon hurried away, just as the Harpist arrived with a group of countryfolk. They hastily constructed a stretcher of branches that had been cut down intertwined with brushwood, placed the injured man on it and transported him gently down the hill, under the direction of a mounted huntsman whom the gentry had left behind. The Harpist, quiet and withdrawn, was carrying his damaged instrument, some other people dragged Philine's trunk, while she sauntered on afterwards carrying a bundle, and Mignon kept on leaping ahead or to one side through bushes and trees, looking longingly at her sick protector.

The latter lay quietly on the stretcher, wrapped in his warm overcoat. An electric warmth seemed to flow over to his body from the fine wool; in any case, he felt put into the most delightful of moods. The overcoat's beautiful owner had made a powerful impression upon him. He could still see the coat falling from her shoulders, and standing before him the noblest figure, surrounded by rays of light; his imagination hastened through cliffs and forests after the one who had disappeared.

It was not until nightfall that the procession arrived at the village in front of the inn where the rest of the company were gathered, bemoaning their irreplaceable losses in tones of despair. The only small public room of the house was crowded with people; some lay on the straw, others occupied the seats, others again had made themselves scarce behind the stove, and in a small room nearby Madame Melina was fearfully awaiting her confinement. Shock had hastened the onset of labour, and with the support provided by the innkeeper's wife, who was a young and inexperienced person, prospects were hardly promising.

When the new arrivals asked to be admitted, there was a general grumbling. It was now contended that it was only on Wilhelm's advice and at his particular direction that the company had taken this dangerous way and had exposed themselves to this mishap. He was held responsible for the unhappy outcome, and they resisted his coming in at the door, maintaining that he would have to try to find accommodation elsewhere. Philine was treated in an even more unfriendly manner; the Harpist and Mignon had to put up with their share of unpleasantness as well.

The huntsman who had been earnestly enjoined by his beautiful mistress to look after those who had been left behind, did not listen to the altercation with patience for long; he set about the company with curses and threats, and ordered them to move closer together and make room for the new arrivals. People started to comply. He prepared for Wilhelm a place on a table, which he pushed into a corner; Philine arranged for her trunk to be placed by the side of it and sat down on the trunk. Everyone squeezed up as best they could, and the huntsman went off to see whether he could not arrange more comfortable accommodation for the couple.

He had scarcely left when the animosity once more made itself heard, and a series of reproaches followed. Everyone talked of his losses and exaggerated them; people inveighed against the boldness which had led to so much suffering and deprivation, they did not even conceal the malicious pleasure which they felt on account of our friend's injuries, and they jeered at Philine, trying to make a crime out of the way she was said to have saved her trunk. From the various taunts and suggestive remarks it was implied that while the plundering and the defeat of the troupe were taking place she had tried to gain the favour of the leader of the robber-band and that she had persuaded him to spare her trunk, who knows by what arts and complaisance. She was said to have been missing for a time. She gave no answer and simply made a clattering noise with the big locks on her trunk, in order to convince envious persons all the more that it was really there and to deepen the despair of the crowd by her own good fortune.

Chapter Eight

Although the considerable loss of blood had made him weak and the appearance of that ministering angel had induced in him a quiet and gentle mood, Wilhelm could not in the end restrain his annoyance at the hard and unjust comments which the discontented company renewed again and again while he remained silent. At last he felt strong enough to draw himself up and to confront them with the rudeness with which they were harassing their friend and leader. He lifted up his bandaged head, supporting himself with some trouble and leaning against the wall, and began to speak with these words:

'I can forgive the grief which everyone feels about his losses and which causes you to insult me at a moment when you should be feeling sorry for me, and which makes you resist me and repulse me the first time that I might expect help from you. Up to now I have considered myself to be rewarded enough by your gratitude and your friendly behaviour for the services which I rendered you and for the favours I showed you; don't mislead me, don't compel me to retrace my steps and go over again in my mind the things that I have done for you; it would only be painful for me to work this out. Chance led me to you, circumstances and a secret inclination have kept me with you. I have shared in your work and in your pleasures; what little I know has been available to you. If you reproach me in a bitter manner for this mishap which has befallen us, you are failing to remember that the first suggestion of taking this route came from strangers and was considered by all of you and approved by everyone as well as by me. If your journey had been completed satisfactorily, everyone would be congratulating themselves for having had the good idea of recommending and preferring this particular way; they would be happy to recall our discussions and the use they made of their votes; now you are making me alone responsible, you are forcing upon me a burden of guilt which I would willingly take over, if it were not that the most genuine sense of conviction cleared me of responsibility, indeed if it were not that I could call upon you yourselves. If you have anything to say against me, present it in an orderly manner, and I shall be able to defend myself; if you have nothing of substance to bring forward, keep quiet and don't torture me now when I am so much in need of rest.'

Instead of giving a reply the girls began to weep once more and to go into their losses in detail; Melina was completely beside himself; for indeed he had suffered most deprivation, more in fact than we can conceive. He stumbled this way and that like a madman in the narrow room, knocking his head against the wall, and cursing and swearing in the most unseemly manner; and when now the innkeeper's wife came out of the small room at the same time with the news that his wife had been delivered of a still-born child, he gave vent to the most impassioned outbursts, and along with these there was a general confusion of weeping, shouting, grumbling and uproar.

In spite of his bodily weakness Wilhelm, who was deeply stirred within himself both with pitying sympathy for their condition and with annoyance because of their petty-minded disposition, felt the whole strength of his soul to be alive. 'I almost feel contempt for you,' he cried out, 'pitiable though you may be. No misfortune justifies us in burdening an innocent person with reproaches; if I have my share of responsibility in this false step that was taken, I have my share of suffering as well. I am lying here wounded, and if the company has had losses, I have lost the most. The pillaging of costumes and the destruction of sets was at my expense; for you Melina, haven't paid me yet, and herewith I release you completely from this obligation.'

'It's all very well for you to be giving things away that no one will ever see again,' cried Melina. 'Your money was in my wife's trunk, and it's your fault that you have lost it. But if only that were everything!' He started afresh to stamp and rage and shout. Everyone remembered the fine clothes from the Count's wardrobe, the buckles, watches, snuff-boxes and hats, for which Melina had traded so well with the valet. At the same time they all once more remembered their own, though much slighter, treasures; they looked with annoyance at Philine's trunk, indicating to Wilhelm that he had indeed not done at all badly by associating with this beauty and by saving his belongings as well by means of her good fortune.

'Do you really believe,' he finally cried out, 'that I shall have anything of my own as long as you are in need, and is it in fact the first occasion in a time of trouble that I have honestly divided what I have with you? Let the trunk be opened, and whatever is mine I will put out for general use.'

'It's *my* trunk,' said Philine, 'and I shan't open it until it suits me. The few oddments of yours that I kept for you can't amount to very much, even if they are sold to the most honest of Jews. Think of yourself, think what it will cost to cure you, and think what can come upon you in a strange land.'

'Philine, you won't keep back from me anything that is mine,' Wilhelm replied, 'and what little there is will save us from immediate embarrassment. But a man possesses quite a lot of other things with which he can assist his friends, and these things don't exactly need to be ready money. My whole being should be devoted to these unfortunate people who, once they have come to themselves again, will regret their present behaviour. Yes,' he continued, 'I feel that you are in need, and I will do all I can for you; give me your trust again, calm yourselves for the time being, accept what I promise you! Who is willing to receive the commitment from me in the name of you all?'

At this he stretched out his hand and cried: 'I promise that I will not withdraw from you or leave you until each one sees his loss doubly or triply repaid, until you have completely forgotten the condition in which you are now, whoever may be responsible for this, and have exchanged this situation with a happier one.'

He still held his hand outstretched, and nobody was willing to take it. 'I promise yet again,' he cried out, as he sank back on his pillow. They all remained quiet; they were put to shame, but were not consoled, and, sitting on her trunk, Philine cracked some nuts that she had found in her pocket.

Chapter Nine

The huntsman came back with some people and made arrangements for removing the wounded man. He had persuaded the local pastor to receive the couple; Philine's trunk was carried off, and she followed with natural decorum. Mignon ran ahead, and when the sick man arrived at the pastor's house, a big double-bed, that had been standing ready for a long time to receive a guest of honour, was provided for him. It was not until now that it was noticed that the wound had opened and had been bleeding considerably. A fresh dressing would be needed. The patient became feverish, Philine nursed him faithfully, and when tiredness overcame her, the Harpist took her place; with the firm intention of keeping watch, Mignon had gone to sleep in a corner.

In the morning, when he had recovered a little, Wilhelm learnt from the huntsman that the gentry who had come to their assistance yesterday had left their estates a short while earlier in order to escape from the disturbances of the war and to reside in a quieter area until peace returned. He referred to the oldish man and his niece, indicating the place where they had first gone to, and explained to Wilhelm how the young lady had impressed upon him that he should take care of those who had been left behind.

The surgeon came in and interrupted Wilhelm as he was expressing his cordial thanks to the huntsman; he gave a detailed account of the injuries, and made the assurance that they would heal easily if the patient would keep still and wait.

After the huntsman had ridden away, Philine explained that he had left with her a purse containing twenty *louis d'ors*, that he had given the churchman a little something for the accommodation and had deposited with him a sum for the medical expenses. It was generally assumed that she was Wilhelm's wife, and she would not hear of his looking around for any other attendant.

'Philine,' said Wilhelm, 'I already owe you a great deal in connection with the misfortune that has overtaken us, and I wouldn't like to see my obligation to you increased. I am restless as long as you are around me; for I don't know how I can repay you for your trouble. Give me my things, which you rescued in your trunk, join the rest of the company, find somewhere else to stay, and take my thanks and the gold watch as a small expression of my appreciation; only do leave me; your presence disturbs me more than you think.'

She laughed in his face when he had finished. 'You are a fool,' she said, 'you just won't be sensible. I know best what is good for you; I'm going to stay. I shan't move from the spot. I've never reckoned with the gratitude of men, and therefore not with yours either; and if I am fond of you, what is it to do with you?'

She stayed and had soon made herself popular with the pastor and his family; she was always cheerful, could give something to everybody and could talk in a way that suited everyone, and at the same time always did what she wanted. Wilhelm was not in a bad state; the surgeon, an uninformed but not unskilful man, let nature take her course, and so the patient was soon on the way to recovery. The latter greatly desired to be restored to health, in order to be able to pursue his aims with zeal.

He kept on recalling that event which had made an indelible impression upon his mind. He saw the beautiful Amazon come riding out of the bushes, she approached him, dismounted, went up and down, and took trouble on his behalf. He saw the enveloping coat fall from her shoulders and saw her face and figure disappear in a glow. All his youthful dreams attached themselves to this vision. He now believed that he had seen with his own eyes the noble and heroic Clorinda; he thought once more of the sick prince, at whose bedside the beautiful, sympathetic princess appears in quiet modesty.

'Might it not be that the visions of future events hover about us in our early years as if in sleep and become visible to our untutored eyes in an anticipatory way?' he said on various occasions in solitude to himself. 'Might not the seeds of what will befall us in the future already be scattered by the hand of fate, and might not an anticipated enjoyment of the fruits that we hope to pluck be possible?'

His bed of sickness gave him the time to go over that scene a thousand times. He recalled the sound of that sweet voice a thousand times; and how he envied Philine who had kissed that helpful hand. The incident often seemed to him like a dream, and he would have thought of it as a fairy-tale, if there had not remained the coat which assured him of the certainty of the appearance.

Combined with the most concerned care for this garment was linked the most eager impulse to put it on and wear it. No sooner had he got up than he clad himself in it and was fearful the whole day through that it might be marked by a stain or damaged in some other way.

Chapter Ten

Laertes visited his friend. He had not been present during that lively scene in the inn, since he had been in an upstairs room. He soon consoled himself about what he had lost and found help in his usual phrase: 'what does it matter?' He spoke of various ridiculous features of the company's behaviour, and in particular he blamed Madame Melina, claiming that she was sorry for the loss of her daughter only because she could not now have the age old German pleasure of christening her by the name of Mechthilde. As far as her husband was concerned, he said that it now was becoming clear that he had had a lot of money with him and that even earlier he had by no means needed the advance which he had wheedled out of Wilhelm. Melina was said now to be going off by the next mail coach and would be asking Wilhelm for a letter of recommendation to his friend the theatre director Serlo, in whose company he now hoped to find a place, since his own undertaking had failed.

Mignon was very quiet for some days, and when she was pressed, she finally confessed that her right arm was dislocated. 'That's the fault of your own recklessness,' Philine said, relating how the child had drawn her hunting-knife in the course of the fighting and had bravely gone for the robbers when she had seen that her friend was in danger. Finally she had been caught by the arm and flung to one side. She was scolded for not having come forward about the injury earlier, though it had been noticed that she had been reluctant to come before the surgeon who up to now had always taken her for a boy. They tried to make good the injury, and she had to have her arm in a sling. She was sensitive again about this, since it meant that she had to leave to Philine the major part of the nursing care in connection with her friend

Wilhelm, and the sweet sinner only showed herself the more active and attentive on that account.

One morning when Wilhelm awoke he found that he was strangely close to her. In the restlessness of his sleep he had slid wholly on to the rear side of the big bed. Philine lay stretched diagonally across the front part; she appeared to have fallen asleep while sitting and reading on the bed. A book had fallen from her hand, and she had sunk back with her head near to his breast over which her fair, unravelled hair was spread flowingly. The disorder of sleep heightened her charms more than art and intention could have done; a childlike, smiling calm was poised about her face. He looked at her for a time and seemed to be reproaching himself for the pleasure with which he regarded her, and we do not know whether he blessed or cursed the condition he was in, which prescribed for him quiet and restraint as a duty. He had been contemplating her attentively for a while when she began to stir. He gently closed his eyes, but he could not stop himself from blinking and looking at her as she tidied herself up again and went off to inquire about breakfast.

By now all the actors had in turn called on Wilhelm, had requested letters of recommendation and travelling expenses in a manner that was more or less clumsy and vehement, and had received them always in the face of Philine's objections. It was in vain that she told her friend that the huntsman had left a respectable sum of money for these people as well, and that Wilhelm was only being hoodwinked. Indeed they quarrelled sharply about this, and Wilhelm now asserted once and for all that she too should join with the rest of the company and try her luck with Serlo.

She lost her equanimity only for a few moments, then she pulled herself quickly together and cried: 'if I only had my blonde boy again, I wouldn't bother about any of you.' She was thinking of Friedrich who had disappeared from the battlefield and not shown himself since.

Next morning Mignon brought the news to Wilhelm, as he lay in bed, that Philine had gone away in the night; he was told that she had placed everything that belonged to him very neatly together. He missed her; he had lost in her going a faithful nurse and a cheerful companion; he was no longer accustomed to being alone. However, Mignon soon filled the gap.

During the time when that frivolous beauty had been enveloping the wounded man with her friendly care, the little one had gradually withdrawn and had remained quietly on her own; but now that she had the field to herself again, she came forward with attentiveness and love, and was keen to serve him and in good spirits for entertaining him.

Chapter Eleven

He was making vigorous steps towards recovery; he hoped now that he could set out on his journey in a few days. He had no wish to continue a drifting and aimless way of life, as it were, instead purposeful steps should mark his path in future. First of all he intended to call on the helpful noble family in order to express his gratitude, and then to hasten to his friend the theatre-manager so that he could look after the company that had come to grief, and at the same time visit the business friends, for whom he had been provided with addresses, and carry out the tasks that had been assigned to him. He was hopeful that good fortune would support him in the future, as had been the case in the past, and provide him with the opportunity of making good the losses by means of a happy piece of speculation, and of replenishing his finances once more.

The wish to see again the one who had saved him grew every day. In order to decide his itinerary, he asked for advice from the pastor who had a good knowledge of geography and statistics and possessed a pleasant collection of books and maps. They looked for the place which the noble family had chosen for their seat during the war period, and they tried to get information about the family itself; but the place was not to be found in any geography book nor on any map, and the genealogical reference works had nothing to say about such a family.

Wilhelm became restless, and when he gave voice to his anxiety, the Harpist revealed to him that he had reason to believe that the huntsman, whatever the grounds might be, had concealed the family's true name.

Wilhelm, who did in fact believe that he was not far from the beautiful lady, hoped to have some news of her if he sent the Harpist to find her; but this hope too was shattered. Although the old man inquired diligently, he failed to find any clues. In those particular days there had been various active movements of people and unforeseen passages of troops through the district; nobody had paid particular attention to that group of travellers, and so the messenger, in order not to be taken for a Jewish spy, had to come back and appear before his master and friend without any olive-branch. He gave a conscientious account of how he had tried to carry out his commission and was strenuously concerned to ward off from himself any suspicion of negligence. He tried to alleviate Wilhelm's depression in all sorts of ways, recalling everything that he had learnt from the huntsman, and came out with a number of suppositions, as a result of which there finally emerged a fact enabling Wilhelm to give a meaning to some mysterious words spoken by the beautiful lady who had now disappeared.

The robber-band had in fact not been lying in wait for the itinerant theatre-company, but for the gentry; they rightly supposed that the aristocratic party had a lot of money and valuables, and they must have had exact information about their expedition. It was not known whether the attack should be ascribed to a volunteer corps or to marauders or robbers. In any case it was a matter of good luck for the elegant and rich caravan that the insignificant and the poor had come to that particular place and had suffered the fate that had been prepared for the others. That was the point of those words spoken by the young lady which Wilhelm still remembered well. If now he could be cheerful and happy because a providential spirit had determined him to be the sacrifice that should save a perfect mortal woman, on the other hand he was close to despair since he had lost all hope of finding and seeing her again, at least for the time being.

What increased this strange movement within him was the similarity which he believed he had discovered between the Countess and the beautiful stranger. They resembled each other like sisters in whose case neither may be called the younger or the older, since they appear to be twins.

The memory of the gracious Countess was infinitely delightful to him. He was only too glad to bring back her picture to his mind. But now the figure of the noble Amazon came immediately in between, and one vision merged into the other without his being in a position to hold firmly to this one or that.

How strange therefore did it seem to him that there was a similarity in their handwriting. For he had in his writing-case a charming song written in the Countess' hand, and he found in the overcoat a note in which someone inquired about an uncle's health with much gentle concern.

Wilhelm was convinced that this rescuer had written this message and that it had been sent from one room to another in an inn during the course of the journey and had been put into the pocket by the uncle. He compared the two handwritings, and while the daintily placed letters of the Countess had formerly pleased him so very much, he discovered in the similar but freer characters of the unknown lady an ineffably flowing harmony. The note said nothing, and yet the strokes of the pen alone appeared to have an inspiring effect upon him, as the presence of the beautiful person had done earlier.

He fell into a mood of rêverie and longing, and the song which Mignon and the Harpist were singing most expressively at this hour as an irregular duet was in harmony with his feelings:

> He alone who knows yearning
> Knows what I suffer.
> Wholly undiscerning
> Of all kinds of joy,
> I look to the sky above
> Over on that side.
> Ah, he who knows me and shows love
> Is far away.
> I swoon, there is a burning
> In my inner being.
> He alone who knows yearning
> Knows what I suffer.

Chapter Twelve

The gentle attractions of the beloved protective spirit, instead of directing our friend upon any specific way, nurtured and increased the disquiet which he had expressed earlier. A secret fire crept into his veins, while images that were both definite and vague alternated in his mind, arousing in him an unending longing. Now he would wish for a horse, now for wings, and while he believed that it was impossible for him to stay, he was only at the stage of looking around and wondering where his impulses might lead him.

Fate's thread had become so strangely confused; he wanted to see the strange knots unravelled or else cut. Often when he heard a horse's trot or the trundling of a coach, he would look hastily out of the window in the hope that it would be someone to visit him and to bring him information, certainty and joy, even if this should only be by chance. He made up stories for himself; how his friend Werner might come into this district and pay him a surprise visit, and how Mariane might perhaps appear. The sound of every postilion's horn agitated him. Melina was supposed to be giving information about what was happening to him, but in particular the huntsman might return and invite him to join the adored beautiful lady.

Unfortunately nothing of all this happened, and in the end he had to continue on his own once more; as he went over past events again, one feature became more and more repugnant and unbearable, the more he looked at it and brought light upon it. This was the mishap that had befallen the company under his leadership, which he could not think of without annoyance. For although he had made more or less adequate excuses for himself to the company on the evening of that evil day, he could none the less not deny his own guilt to himself. In fact, in moments of hypochondria he ascribed to himself the whole responsibility for the event.

Self-love causes us to see our virtues as well as our faults as being more significant than they are. He had caused people to have confidence in him, had directed the will of the rest of the party, and had gone on ahead, led by inexperience and boldness; they had been involved in a danger which they could not cope with. He was pursued by reproaches that were both voiced and silent, and in assuring the misled troupe after their heavy loss that he would not leave them until he had made good the loss with interest, he now had to reproach himself for a further rash act with which he was presuming to take upon his own shoulders a misfortune that had been distributed among the group. Sometimes he reproved himself for having given such a promise because of tension and under the stress of the moment; at other times he felt that the good-natured proffering of his hand, which no one had deigned to accept, had only been a light formality compared to the promise made by his heart. He tried to think of ways in which he could be beneficent and useful to them, and found good reason for hastening on his journey to Serlo. So he packed up his things and, without waiting until he was fully recovered or listening to the advice of the pastor and the surgeon, he hurried off in the strange company of Mignon and the old man in order to escape from the inactivity to which his fate had once more confined him only too long.

Chapter Thirteen

Serlo received him with open arms and called out to him: 'Is it you? Do I recognize you again? You haven't changed much, perhaps not at all. Is your love of the noblest of arts still as keen and live? I am so pleased at your arrival that I don't even feel any longer the mistrust which your last letters aroused in me.'

Taken aback, Wilhelm asked for an explanation.

'You haven't been acting towards me like an old friend,' Serlo rejoined. 'You have been treating me like some great gentleman to whom useless people may be recommended with a good conscience. Our fate is dependent on public opinion, and I'm afraid that your Mr. Melina and his people would be hardly likely to get a good reception here.'

Wilhelm was about to say something in their favour, but Serlo began to portray them in such unmerciful terms that our friend was very pleased when a lady came into the room, interrupted the conversation and was introduced to him by Serlo as the latter's sister Aurelia. She welcomed him in the most friendly manner and her conversation was so agreeable that he did not even perceive the marked line of grief that gave her intelligent features a further special interest.

It was the first occasion for a long time that Wilhelm again found that he was in his element. Hitherto in his conversations he had only found listeners who were just adequately pleasing; now he had the good fortune to be talking with artists and connoisseurs who not only understood him perfectly but could respond instructively to his words as well. How rapidly they went through the latest plays! How surely they passed judgement on them! How accurately they could examine and appreciate the public's viewpoint! With what speed could they explain things to each other!

With Wilhelm's particular liking for Shakespeare, conversation now turned to this writer of necessity. He demonstrated the most eager expectations with regard to the impact that these fine plays would be bound to make in Germany, and it was not long before he came out with his *Hamlet* that had been preoccupying him so much.

Serlo assured him that he would have put on the play a long time before this, if it had only been possible, and that he would be glad to take the part of Polonius. Then he added with a smile: 'And Ophelias can be found too, once we've got the Prince of Denmark.'

Wilhelm did not notice that Aurelia did not seem to like this joke of her brother's; in fact he became expansive and didactic in his way on the subject of how he would like to see Hamlet played. He expounded in detail the conclusions with which we have seen him preoccupied earlier, and made every effort to present his opinion in a pleasing way, however many doubts Serlo might express about his hypothesis. 'All right then,' Serlo finally said, 'we will grant you all this; what more do you want to deduce from it?'

'A great deal, everything,' Wilhelm replied. 'Imagine a prince, as I have described him, whose father unexpectedly dies. Ambition and power are not the passions that motivate him; he had been satisfied to be a king's son; but now for the first time he is compelled to take more account of the gulf that separates the king from his subjects. The right to the crown was not hereditary, but if his father had lived longer, the claims of the only son would have been further strengthened and his hope of the crown ensured. But now he sees himself excluded, perhaps for ever, by his uncle in spite of apparent promises; he now feels so lacking in favour and material goods, and a stranger in a place that he had been able to regard as his own property from his early years on. At this point his temperament takes its first melancholy direction. He feels that he is no more than any nobleman, indeed not as much; he sees himself as being at everyone's beck and call, he is not polite and gracious, on the contrary, he is deprived and needy.

'He looks back at his earlier position as if only to a vanished dream. It is in vain that his uncle attempts to cheer him up and show him his position from a different point of view; the feeling of his own nothingness never leaves him.

'The second blow to befall him struck harder, bowed him down even more. That is, his mother's marriage. When his father died there remained still a mother for the loyal and tender son; he hoped that in the company of his noble widowed mother he would be able to revere the heroic figure of that great departed man; but he loses his mother as well, and it is worse than if she had been snatched from him by death. The reliable picture which a well-bred child so much likes to have of his parents disappears; there is no help to be had from the dead man, and no stable hold from the living woman. She is a woman as well, and she too is comprised in the general name applied to her sex, frailty.

'Now for the first time he feels really bowed down, really orphaned, and no happiness in the world can replace to him what he has lost. Not melancholy and introspective by nature, sadness and reflection become a heavy burden for him. This is how we see

him on the stage. I don't think that I am interpreting anything
into the play or exaggerating any aspect.'

Serlo looked at his sister and said: 'Was I wrong in the
impression I gave you of our friend? He's starting off well, and
will have quite a number of things still to tell us and a lot to
persuade us of.' Wilhelm swore by all that was holy that he did
not wish to persuade, but to convince, and asked only that they
should be patient a little while longer.

'Just think of this young man, this monarch's son, in clear
terms,' he cried, 'imagine his position, and then watch him when
he learns that the figure of his father is to appear; stand by him in
the fearful night when the venerable ghost itself is to step forth.
He is seized by a monstrous terror; he speaks to the miraculous
shape, sees it beckon, follows and listens. His ears resound with
the most terrible accusation against his uncle, with the demand
for revenge, and with the urgent, repeated request: "remember
me"!

'And when the ghost has disappeared, whom do we see standing
before us? A young hero breathing revenge? A born monarch who
feels happy at being summoned against the usurper of his crown?
No! Astonishment and gloom befall the solitary prince; he
becomes bitter against the smiling villains, swears that he will not
forget the one who has departed, and closes with the significant
expression of dismay: "The time is out of joint: O cursed spite,
that ever I was born to set it right!"

'It is in these words, I think, that the key to Hamlet's whole
behaviour lies, and it is clear to me that what Shakespeare wanted
to describe was: a great deed laid upon a person who was not
equal to it. And I see the play as consistently constructed with this
in mind. An oak-tree is here planted in an exquisite vessel that
should only have received sweet flowers into its bosom; the roots
spread, and the vessel is destroyed.

'A fine, pure, noble, most highly moral person, lacking the
sensuous strength that makes a hero, collapses beneath a burden
that he can neither bear nor throw off; all duty is sacred to him,
but this obligation is too heavy. The impossible is being asked of
him, not the impossible in itself, but what is impossible for him.
How he twists and turns, fears, steps back and forth, is constantly
reminded, reminds himself constantly, and in the end almost loses
sight of his purpose, though without ever becoming happy again!'

Chapter Fourteen

Various persons came in, interrupting the talk. They were musicians who usually came together once a week at Serlo's for a little music-making. He loved music very much and maintained that without this love an actor could never acquire a clear understanding and feeling for his own art. Just as movement is much easier and becoming when gestures are accompanied and led by melody, so too the actor has, as it were, to compose his prose part in his mind, so that he does not monotonously botch the role in his own particular way, but handles it in appropriate modulation according to time and measure.

Aurelia seemed to take little interest in all that was going on, in fact she finally led our friend to a side-room, saying to him, as she went to a window and looked up at the starry sky: 'You have still further things to say to us about Hamlet; now, I don't want to be over-hasty and I would like my brother also to hear what you have to say to us further, but do let me hear your thoughts about Ophelia.'

'There's not much to say about her,' Wilhelm replied, 'for her character had been completed just with a few master-strokes. Her whole being hovers in a mature, sweet sensuousness. Her affection for the prince, on whose hand in marriage she may lay claim, flows so sincerely, and her fond heart surrenders so completely to its desire, that both her father and her brother are afraid, and both speak out their warnings directly, indeed immodestly. Well-being, like the light gauze on her bosom, cannot conceal the movement of her heart, indeed it is an indicator of this gentle motion. Her imagination is set on fire, her quiet modesty is suffused by loving desire, and if the easy-going goddess of opportunity were to shake the little tree, the fruit would at once fall off.'

'And then,' said Aurelia, 'when she sees herself deserted, rejected and despised, when in her mad lover's soul the highest descends to the depths, and when he offers her not the sweet goblet of love but the bitter cup of suffering –'

'Her heart breaks,' Wilhelm cried out, 'the whole framework of her existence is dislocated, her father's death rushes upon her, and the lovely structure collapses completely.'

Wilhelm had not noticed how much expression Aurelia put into her last words. Directing his attention only on to the work of art, its coherence and perfection, he did not realize that his companion was experiencing quite different feelings, and that a deep private sorrow was being aroused within her by these dramatic phantoms.

Aurelia's head, supported by her arms, and her eyes which were filled with tears were still turned towards the sky. At last she could no longer restrain her concealed grief; she grasped Wilhelm's two hands and cried out, as he stood in surprise before her: 'Please forgive a fearful heart! Society strangles and confines me; I have to try to hide myself from my merciless brother; your presence now has loosened all bonds. My friend!' she went on, 'we have only been acquainted for a moment, and already I am confiding in you.' She could scarcely utter the words, and she sank upon his shoulder. 'Don't think any the worse of me,' she said sobbing, 'because I am revealing myself to you so quickly, and because you see me in such a weak state. Be my friend, stay my friend, I deserve this.' He spoke to her in very heartfelt tones, but it was in vain; her tears flowed and smothered her words.

At this moment Serlo made a very unwelcome appearance and Philine, whose hand he was holding, made a very unexpected one. 'Here's your friend,' he said to her; 'he will be pleased to greet you.'

'What!' cried Wilhelm in surprise, 'are you here?' She went up to him with modest, sedate demeanour, welcomed him, commended the generosity of Serlo who had taken her into his fine company without any merit on her part, merely in the hope that she would develop. In saying this, she behaved to Wilhelm in a friendly manner, but from a respectful distance.

This pretence, however, only lasted as long as Serlo and Aurelia were present. For after Aurelia had disappeared in order to conceal her sorrow and Serlo had been called away, Philine first checked the doors carefully to see that the two had gone for certain, then she hopped like mad around the room, sat down on the floor and almost choked with giggling and laughing. Then she sprang up, caressed our friend and expressed her extreme satisfaction that she had been sensible enough to go ahead, spy out the land and make herself at home.

'It's pretty lively here,' she said, 'just the way I like it. Aurelia has had an unhappy love-affair with a nobleman who must be a first-rate person and whom I should like to see myself some time. He has left her something to remember him by, or else I'm much mistaken. There's a boy running around, about three years old, as pretty as a picture; his papa must be a poppet. I can't stand children usually, but I like this lad. I've worked it out as far as she's concerned. Her husband's death, the new acquaintance, the child's age, it all fits.

'Now the lover has made off; she hasn't seen him for a year.

She is beside herself and inconsolable about it. The fool! The brother has a dancing girl in the troupe with whom he is doing nicely, and a little actress with whom he is intimate, and in the town a few women to whom he pays attention, and now I'm on the list as well. The fool! You shall hear about the rest of the people tomorrow. And now one more little word from Philine, whom you know: this out-and-out fool has fallen in love with you.' She swore that it was true and avowed that it was great fun. She implored Wilhelm to fall in love with Aurelia; then the chase would be really on. 'She would run after her unfaithful lover, you would run after her, I would run after you, and her brother after me. If this doesn't provide six months of entertainment, I will die at the first episode which comes to be added to this fourfold intertwined romance.' She begged him not to spoil her sport and to show her as much respect as she would merit with her public behaviour.

Chapter Fifteen

The next morning Wilhelm intended to visit Madame Melina; he did not find her at home, inquired about the other members of the itinerant company, and learned that Philine had invited them to breakfast. Out of curiosity he hurried there and found them all in good spirits and in conciliated mood. The clever creature had brought them together, served them with chocolate and given them to understand that all doors were not as yet closed; she had said that she hoped to use her influence to convince the director how advantageous it would be for him to take on such able people in his company. They listened to her attentively, drank noisily one cup of chocolate after another, thought that the girl was not at all bad, and resolved to speak very well of her.

'Do you actually believe that Serlo may still decide to keep our companions on?' Wilhelm said, having stayed behind on his own with Philine. 'Not at all,' Philine rejoined, 'nor is it of any importance to me; I wish they would go away, the sooner the better! I would like to keep just Laertes; we shall get rid of the rest little by little.'

At this point she intimated to her friend that she was certainly convinced that now he would no longer be burying his talents, but that under Serlo's direction he would go on the stage. She could not find enough praise for the order, good taste and thought that were said to predominate here; she spoke so fondly to our friend, talking in such flattering terms about his talents, that his heart and imagination felt as much drawn to this proposal as his reason and judgment shrank from it. He concealed his inclination from himself and from Philine, and had a restless day during which he could not make up his mind to going to his commercial correspondents' to collect any letters that might be waiting for him there. For although he could imagine his relatives' disquiet during this time, he was reluctant to learn in detail about their worries and to receive their reproaches, the more so as he was looking forward with great and unalloyed pleasure to the performance of a new play that evening.

Serlo had refused to admit him to rehearsals. 'You will first have to get to know us in the best light before you see what we're up to.'

It was therefore with the greatest satisfaction that our friend attended the performance on the following evening. All the actors could be confidently expected to have excellent gifts, happy temperaments and a high, clear conception of their art, and yet they were not like each other; but they took care of themselves and supported each other in turn, urged each other on, and in their whole performance were very definite and precise. It could soon be sensed that Serlo was the heart and soul of everything, and he showed himself very much to his advantage. He had to be admired for his gaiety of mood, his controlled vivacity, his definite feeling for what is appropriate and at the same time his great imitative talent, for the way he appeared on the stage and the way he opened his mouth. The relaxed quality of his inner self seemed to extend to all the audience, and the intelligent way in which he found easy and pleasing expression for the most subtle nuances in the parts aroused all the more delight as he knew how to conceal the art which he had made his own through continual practice.

His sister Aurelia equalled him and received even louder applause, since she stirred peoples' emotions while he was able to bring gaiety and pleasure.

After a few days spent in an agreeable way, Aurelia requested our friend's presence. He hurried to her and found her reclining on the sofa; she seemed to be suffering from headache, and her whole self could not conceal her feverish movement. Her eyes lit up when she saw him coming in. 'Do forgive me!' she called to him, 'the confidence that you inspired in me has made me weak. Up to now I have been able to pass the time quietly with my sorrows, indeed, they gave me strength and consolation; now, I don't know how it has happened, you have loosened the bonds of reticence, and now you will have to take part, even against your will, in the struggle which I fight against myself.'

Wilhelm answered in a friendly and courteous manner. He assured her that her image and her sorrows had been hovering constantly before his soul, that he wished that she would be trusting to him, and that he should dedicate himself to being her friend.

Speaking thus, his eyes were attracted by the boy who was sitting on the ground in front of her and throwing all sorts of toys about. As Philine had already indicated, he might be about three years old, and Wilhelm now understood for the first time why the frivolous girl, who was seldom elevated in her expressions, compared the boy to the sun. For the most beautiful golden locks fell in curls around the frank, brown eyes and the full face, and delicate, dark, gently arched eyebrows stood out against a dazzling white forehead, while the lively colour of good health shone upon his cheeks. 'Sit down by me,' said Aurelia; 'you are looking at the happy child in surprise; certainly, I have gladly taken him into my arms, and I look after him with care; only I can also measure against him the extent of my sorrows, for these only rarely allow me to appreciate the value of such a gift.

'Allow me now to say something also about myself and my fate,' she continued; 'for it is very important to me that you should not misunderstand me. I thought I had a few quiet moments, that's why I had you summoned; now you are here, and I've lost the thread of what I wanted to say.

'"One more deserted creature in the world!" you will say. You are a man and you think: "What a fuss she is making about a necessary evil that hovers over a woman, the little fool, more certainly than death, that is, the infidelity of a man!" Oh, my friend, if my fate were a common one, I would gladly put up with common misfortune; but it is so extraordinary; why can't I show it to you in the mirror, why not give someone the task of relating it to you! Oh, if I had simply been seduced, surprised and then left in the lurch, there would then still be consolation in despair; but I am in a far worse position, I have tricked myself, I have deceived myself against my will, that's what I can never forgive myself for.'

'With noble sentiments like yours,' Wilhelm interpolated, 'you can't be wholly unhappy.'

'And do you know what I owe my ways of thinking to?' Aurelia asked; 'to the worst possible education through which a girl could ever have been dragged down, to the worst example that could mislead senses and inclination.

'After my mother's death I spent the most beautiful period of a child's development in the charge of an aunt who made it a law to despise the laws of decent behaviour. She yielded blindly to every inclination, she did not care whether she dominated over the object of her passion or was its slave, so long only as she could forget herself in wild pleasure.

'What ideas concerning the male sex confronted us children with our pure clear gaze of innocence? How dull, pressing, bold and clumsy each man seemed as she enticed him to her; on the other hand, how satiated, empty and vulgar, once his wishes had been satisfied. In this way I have seen this woman for years on end humiliated under the domination of the worst possible people; what encounters she had to put up with, how coolly she took her fate upon herself, indeed, with what style she could bear these shameful fetters!

'That's how I got to know your sex, my friend, and how much I hated it, when I seemed to notice that in their relations with our sex even tolerable men appeared to lose all the feelings of decency which nature might otherwise have made them capable of.

'Unfortunately, in the course of such events I had to come to many sad conclusions about my own sex, and indeed, as a girl of sixteen I was more sensible than I am now, for at present I hardly understand myself. Why are we so sensible when we are young, so sensible, but only to become more and more foolish!'

The boy was making a noise; Aurelia became impatient and rang. An old woman came in to take him away. 'Have you still got tooth-ache?' Aurelia asked the old woman whose face was bound up. 'It's almost unbearable,' the latter replied in a hollow voice; she lifted up the boy, who seemed to be glad to go with her, and took him off.

The child had scarcely left when Aurelia began to cry bitterly. 'I can't do anything but moan and complain,' she cried out, 'and I am ashamed to be prostrate before you like a helpless creature. My composure has already gone, and I can't continue with my story.' She faltered and became silent. Her companion, who was not desirous of saying anything of a general nature and who had nothing specific to put forward, pressed her hand and looked at her for a time. Finally in his embarrassment he picked up a book that he found on the small table in front of him; it was a volume of Shakespeare, opened at *Hamlet*.

Serlo who was just coming in at the door and was asking how his sister felt, looked into the book that our friend was holding in his hand and cried out: 'Do I find you poring over your *Hamlet* again? That's fine! Quite a number of doubts have reached me which seem to reduce very much the canonical respect which you would be so glad to pay to the play. After all, the English themselves have confessed that the main interest finishes with the third act, and that the two last acts only keep the whole together in a pitiful way; and it is indeed true that as the end approaches the play refuses to get moving or make progress.'

'It is very possible,' Wilhelm said, 'that some members of a nation that has so many masterpieces to show are led to false judgments because of their prejudices and limitations; but that can't stop us from seeing with our own eyes and being just. I am far from blaming the construction of this play, I believe rather that no greater plot has ever been thought out; indeed, it has not been thought out, it simply is like that.'

'How do you intend to explain that?' asked Serlo.

'I don't want to explain anything,' replied Wilhelm, 'I just want to put before you what I have been thinking.'

Aurelia raised herself up from her cushion, supported herself on her hand and looked at our friend who, with the greatest conviction that he was right, went on talking in this way: 'It pleases and flatters us so much when we see a hero who acts on his own account, loving and hating when his heart commands, who makes plans and carries them out, who overcomes all obstacles and comes to the fulfilment of a great purpose. Historians and poets would like to persuade us that such a proud fate can befall man. Here we are taught differently; the hero has no plan, but the play is planned. We don't have here for instance a villain who is punished according to an idea of revenge that is put into effect in a rigid and headstrong manner, no, a monstrous deed takes place which is continuing in its consequences and which drags along the innocent in its wake; the criminal seems to want to avoid the abyss that is intended for him and yet plunges in, just when he thinks that his course is working out successfully. For it is in the nature of a horrible deed that it brings evil upon innocent persons too, just as a good deed offers many advantages to the undeserving, without the author of one or the other receiving either reward or punishment. How wonderfully things happen in our play! Purgatory sends forth its ghost and demands revenge, but in vain. All circumstances coincide and drive on to vengeance, but in vain! Neither earthly beings nor those from the underworld can succeed in carrying out what has been reserved for fate alone. The hour of judgment arrives. The evil man falls with the good. One race is mowed down, and another comes in its place.'

After a pause in which they looked at one another, Serlo replied: 'You're not paying any special compliment to Providence by extolling the poet, and then it seems to me that in order to honour your poet, like other people honouring Providence, you are ascribing to him purposes and plans which he never thought of.'

Chapter Sixteen

'Let me put in a question too,' Aurelia said. 'I've had another look at the part of Ophelia, I am content with it and would trust myself to play it under certain circumstances. But tell me, should not the poet have given his mad heroine other songs to sing? Couldn't fragments from sorrowful ballads have been chosen? What are ambiguities and lascivious stupidities doing on the lips of this pure girl?'

'Dear friend,' Wilhelm replied, 'I can't give way an inch here either. There's great meaning even in these eccentricities, even in this apparent impropriety. For after all we know right at the start of the play what is preoccupying the sweet child's mind. She lived quietly, but hardly concealed her yearning and her wishes. The sounds of lasciviousness echoed secretly in her soul, and how often may she not, like an incautious nurse, have tried to lull her sensuality with songs that could not but make it more wakeful. In the end, when she has lost all control of herself and her heart's secrets are hovering upon her tongue, it is this tongue that betrays her, and in the innocence of madness she amuses herself in the presence of the king and the queen with reminiscences from the loose songs she had been fond of: the song about the girl who was overcome, the song about the girl stealing off to her lover, and so on.'

He had scarcely finished these words when all at once there took place before his eyes a strange scene which he could in no way explain.

Serlo had paced a few times up and down the room without permitting any purpose on his part to arouse attention. Suddenly he went up to Aurelia's dressing-table, snatched at something that was lying there, and hurried towards the door with the spoils. As soon as Aurelia noticed his action, she sprang up, obstructed him, attacked him with incredible passion and was dexterous enough to grasp hold of one end of the object that had been taken. They wrestled and scuffled very persistently, writhing and turning around together vigorously; he laughed, she got excited, and when Wilhelm hurried along with the intention of separating them and

calming them down, he saw Aurelia suddenly leap to one side with
a bare dagger in her hand, while Serlo irritably threw to the
ground the sheath which he had been left with. Wilhelm stepped
back in surprise, and his mute astonishment seemed to be asking
why such an unusual struggle about such a strange article could
have arisen among them.

'You can be the umpire between the two of us,' Serlo said.
'What does she want the sharp steel for? Take a look at it. This
dagger isn't suitable for an actress; it's pointed and sharp like
needle and knife! What good is such foolery? Impulsive as she is,
she can again do herself an accidental injury. I have a deep-seated
dislike of such eccentricities; a serious thought on these lines is
mad, and such a dangerous toy is in bad taste.'

'I've got it again!' cried Aurelia, holding the polished blade up
on high; 'I'm going to look after my faithful friend better now.
Pardon me,' she exclaimed, as she kissed the steel, 'for neglecting
you so.'

Serlo seemed to be becoming angry in earnest. 'Take it as you
like, brother,' she continued; 'but can you know that perhaps a
rare talisman has not been granted to me in this form? Does
everything that looks dangerous have to be harmful?'

'That sort of talk, which has no meaning in it, can make me
mad!' said Serlo, and he left the room with repressed anger.
Aurelia carefully put away the dagger in its sheath and kept it on
her person. 'Let us continue the conversation which my unhappy
brother has interrupted,' she interposed, when Wilhelm asked
some questions about the strange struggle.

'I suppose I must not dispute with you about your portrayal of
Ophelia,' she continued; 'I don't want to misunderstand the poet's
intention; only I can regret it rather than sympathize with it. But
now permit me to make an observation, for which you have often
given me the occasion in the short short time we have known each
other. I notice with admiration the profound and true perception
with which you judge literature, and in particular dramatic
writing; the deepest abysses of invention are not hidden from you,
and you are aware of the most subtle aspects of accomplishment.
Without ever having seen the objects in nature, you recognize the
truth in the picture; there seems to be contained within yourself
an anticipatory awareness of the whole world which is stimulated
and developed through the harmonious contact with poetry. For
indeed,' she went on, 'nothing gets through to you from outside; I
have seldom seen anyone who knows the people with whom he is
living as little as you do, who indeed basically misunderstands
them. Allow me to say this: when one hears you expounding your

Shakespeare, it is as if you had just come from the councils of the gods and had been listening to discussions there about the way human beings were to be shaped and formed; but when you are dealing with people, I see you so to speak as the first child of creation, born in adult state, who looks at lions, monkeys, sheep and elephants with particular surprise and instructive amiability and who guilelessly addresses these creatures as beings of his own kind, just because they are there too and can move around.'

'The apprehension about my schoolboyish nature is often troublesome to me, dear friend,' he rejoined, 'and I shall be grateful to you if you will help me to acquire greater clarity concerning the world. From my early years onwards I have directed my mind's eye inward rather than to the outside world, and it is therefore very natural that I have got to know man in general to a certain extent, though without understanding and comprehending people as human beings in the least.'

'It's true,' said Aurelia, 'I suspected you at first of trying to play a practical joke on us, since you had such a lot of good things to say about the people you sent to my brother, when I compared your letters with merits of these people.'

Aurelia's comment, true though it might be and willing though Wilhelm was to concede this failing in himself, none the less had an oppressive, even offensive quality about it, with the result that he became quiet and summoned up all his strength, partly in order not to show any sensitiveness and partly to search within himself for the truth of this reproach.

'You're not to be taken aback,' Aurelia continued; 'we can always acquire the light of understanding, but no one can give us fullness of heart. If you are destined to be an artist, you cannot retain this obscurity and innocence long enough; these are the beautiful covering over the young bud; it is misfortune enough if we are brought into flower too soon. Indeed, it is good if we don't always know the people whom we are working for.

'Oh! I too was once in this happy condition when I stepped on to the stage with the most elevated conception of myself and my nation. What were not the German people in my imagination, and what could they not be! I spoke to this nation over which the small structure of the stage raised me, and from which I was separated by a row of lights whose glitter and fumes prevented me from distinguishing clearly what was in front of me. How I welcomed the sound of applause that came up from the crowd; how gratefully I accepted the gift that was being offered unanimously by so many hands! For a long time I deluded myself along these lines; as I made my impact so the crowd reacted again to me; I was

on the best of terms with my public; I believed that I was
experiencing perfect harmony and that I could see before me in
the audience at all times the noblest and best representatives of
the nation.

'Unfortunately it wasn't the actress' disposition and art alone
that interested theatregoers, they also made claims on the lively
young girl. They intimated to me in no uncertain terms that they
believed that it was my duty to share with them, in a personal
manner too, the emotions that I had aroused in them. Unhappily
this was not my task; I wished to elevate their spirits, but I didn't
lay the slightest claim on what they called their hearts; and so
now all ranks, ages and types of people became burdensome to me,
one after the other, and nothing was more annoying to me than
the fact that I could not shut myself off in my room like any other
honest girl, and thus save myself a lot of trouble.

'The men mostly showed themselves in the way I had got used
to seeing them at my aunt's, and they would again only have
aroused my revulsion this time too, if I had not found their
peculiarities and silliness entertaining. As I couldn't avoid seeing
them now in the theatre, now in public places, and now at home, I
made up my mind to be on the look-out for all of them, and my
brother assisted me resolutely in this. And when you realize that
they all paraded past me in turn, from the nimble shop-assistant
and the conceited merchant's son to the skilful and cautious man
of the world, the bold soldier and the impetuous prince, and that
each of them was hoping to start a romance in his own way, you
will pardon me for imagining that I was pretty well acquainted
with people of my nation.

'The fantastically dressed up student, the man of learning who
is both humble and proud in his self-consciousness, the
unassuming canon with his faltering step, the stiffly attentive
business-man, the rough country squire, the courtier who is
smooth and insipid in a friendly way, the young priest who is
leaving the path he should follow, and merchants who are calm as
well as those who are quick and active in speculation, I have seen
the lot of them in emotional mood, and by heavens, there were few
amongst them who would have been able to stimulate even a
common interest in me; in fact it was most annoying for me to
accept the applause of fools as individuals, for it caused me
trouble and boredom, whereas this applause had pleased me
greatly when it came in the mass, and I had been on the whole so
pleased to claim it for myself then.

'When I was looking for a sensible compliment about my
performance and when I hoped that people would praise an

author whom I esteemed highly, they would make one silly
remark after another and talk about some tasteless play in which
they wanted to see me act. When I listened around in the company
to find out whether there might be some echo of a feature that was
noble, intelligent or witty and which might make its appearance
again at the right time, I could seldom hear any such trace. The
important points for them, which they held on to tightly and from
which they could not get away, were the mistakes that had
happened when an actor spoke his lines wrongly or when he let
slip a dialect word. In the end I did not know which way to turn;
they fancied themselves as being too wise to need entertaining,
and they believed they were entertaining me wonderfully if they
could be petting me. I began to be heartily contemptuous of them
all, and I felt as though the whole nation had quite deliberately
wanted to prostitute itself in my case by means of its
representatives. They seemed to me as a whole to be so gauche, so
badly brought up and educated, so devoid of charm and so lacking
in taste. I often used to exclaim: "No German can even buckle up
a shoe unless he has learnt how from some foreign people!"

'You see how deluded and pathologically unjust I was, and the
longer it went on, the worse my illness became. I could have
committed suicide; only I arrived at another extreme: I got
married, or rather I drifted into a marriage. My brother who had
taken over the theatre very much wished to have an assistant. His
choice fell upon a young man whom I did not dislike and who
lacked everything that my brother possessed: genius, liveliness,
spirit and verve, but who in his turn was endowed with all that
was missing in my brother's case: love of order, industry, and the
valuable gift of being able to be economical and to handle money.

'He became my husband without my knowing how; we had our
life together without my really knowing why. Enough; our affairs
went well. We took in a lot of money, and my brother's activity
was the reason for this; we managed well, and this was my
husband's merit. I gave up thinking about the world and the
nation. When I appeared on the stage, I did so in order to make a
living; I only opened my mouth because I was not allowed to be
silent, because after all I had made my appearance in order to
speak.

'In fact I had surrendered completely to my brother's intentions
and I must not describe the position in too harsh terms; he was
concerned for applause and money; for, between the two of us, he
likes to hear himself praised and spends a lot. I no longer acted in
response to my feelings now, but followed his directions, and if I
had performed in a way that earned his gratitude, I was satisfied.

He adjusted to all the foibles of the public; the money came in, he could live as he wanted, and we had some good times with him.

'Meanwhile I got into a mechanical sort of routine. I dragged out my days without pleasure or sympathetic interest, my marriage was a childless one and only lasted a short time. My husband became ill, his energies declined visibly, and caring for him cut short my general indifference. It was at this time that I met someone with whom a new life began for me, a novel and a faster life, for soon it will be at an end.'

She paused for a time, and then she continued: 'All at once my talkative mood has come to a halt, and I don't trust myself to open my mouth further. Let me rest a little; you are not to go without hearing all about my misfortunes in detail. But in the meantime do call in Mignon and hear what she wants.'

While Aurelia was talking, the child had been into the room several times. As the tone had become quieter when Mignon came in, she had slipped away again, and was sitting quietly waiting in the assembly room. When she was told to come in again, she brought a book with her that could soon be recognized, by its shape and binding, as a small atlas. While staying on the journey with the pastor, she had seen her first maps with great astonishment, had asked him a lot of questions about them and had provided herself with information, as far as was possible. Her desire to learn seemed to be becoming much livelier as a result of this new knowledge. She pleaded with Wilhelm for him to buy her the book. She told him that she had pledged her big silver buckles with the picture-dealer and that she wanted to redeem them first thing in the morning, as it had become so late that evening. She was allowed to do this, and she now began to recite what she knew and also in her usual manner to ask the strangest questions. Here too it could be noticed that although she made great efforts, she only understood things with difficulty and effort. It was similar with her handwriting, which she took a lot of trouble over. She still spoke German in a very broken fashion, and it was only when she opened her mouth to sing and played the zither that she seemed to be using the one organ which enabled her to unlock and reveal her most inward self.

Now that we happen to be talking about her, we must also recall the embarrassment she had frequently been causing to our friend in the recent past. Whenever she came or went, or whenever she said good morning or good night, she enclosed him so firmly in her arms and kissed him with such ardour that he often felt anxiety on account of the intensity of her youthful personality. The convulsive vivacity in her behaviour seemed to increase daily, and her whole being moved in a precarious calm. She could not manage without twisting string in her hands, wringing a piece of cloth or chewing a bit of paper or wood. All her games seemed to serve the purpose only of deflecting an intense inward shock. The only thing that appeared to make her to some extent cheerful was the proximity of little Felix, in whose company she could behave very agreeably.

Aurelia, who after some rest at last felt in the mood for discussing with her friend a subject which was very close to her heart, this time became impatient with the girl's persistence in staying and made it clear to her that she should be off, and in the end, as there was no other alternative, they had to send her away expressly and against her will.

'Now or never,' said Aurelia, 'I must tell you the rest of my story. If my dearly loved, unfair friend were only a few miles from here, I would say: "Mount your horse, try to get to know him in some way or other, and when you return, you will certainly have pardoned me and you will be sorry for him from the bottom of your heart." Now I can only tell you in words how agreeable he was and how much I loved him.

'I first met him just at the critical time when I was forced to be anxious for my husband's life. He had just come back from America, where he had served in company with some Frenchmen with great distinction under the colours of the United States.

'He met me with a calm and pleasing demeanour and with good-natured frankness, talking about myself, my position and my acting like an old acquaintance with such sympathy and insight that for the first time I could be happy to see my own life reflected so clearly in another person. His judgments were correct without being derogatory, and striking without being unkind. He did not show any hardness, and his petulance was at the same time likeable. He seemed to be used to finding favour with women, and this made me watchful; he was not at all ingratiating or pressing, and this made me careless.

'In the town he only went about with a few people, was mostly on horseback, visited his many acquaintances round about and looked after the business affairs of his family household. When he did come back here, he called on us, treated my husband, who was becoming increasingly ill, with tender care, procured the services of a clever doctor, which brought some relief to the patient, and just as he showed sympathetic concern for everything to do with myself, so also I was allowed to share an interest in what had befallen him. He told me the story of his campaign, of the irresistible attraction he felt to the profession of soldier, and of his family circumstances; he confided to me about his present preoccupations. In fact, he had no secrets from me; he unfolded his inmost self to me, and let me see into the most hidden parts of his being; I got to know his capacities and his passions. It was the first time in my life that I could enjoy an association that was cordial and intelligent. I was attracted, indeed enchanted by him before I could take a critical look at myself.

'In the meantime I had lost my husband, rather in the way I had acquired him. The burden of the theatre's business affairs now fell wholly on my shoulders. My brother, although unsurpassable on the stage, was never of use on the management side; I looked after everything and at the same time studied my parts more busily than ever. Once more my acting was as it had been earlier, though in fact filled with quite a different strength and with a new life, through him and on his account, it is true, but I did not always have the greatest success when I knew that my noble friend was in the audience; but there were a few times when he listened to me without my knowing it, and you can imagine what a pleasant surprise his unexpected applause was to me.

'It's true, I'm a strange creature. With every part that I played I actually felt exclusively as if I were praising him and speaking in his honour; for that was the mood of my heart, whatever the spoken words might be in fact. If I knew he was in the audience, I did not trust myself to speak out with entire force, just as though I did not want to force my love and praise upon him; if he wasn't there, I had a free hand, I gave of my best with a certain calm and with a wondrous contentment. I took pleasure at the applause again, and whenever I gave the audience pleasure, I would have liked at the same time to call down to them: "You owe that to him!"

'Yes, indeed, my relationship with the theatre public and to the whole nation had been completely changed, as if by a miracle. All at once the people appeared to me in the most advantageous light again, and I was really surprised at the way I had been deluded hitherto.

'"How lacking in understanding I was when I used to inveigh against the nation, just because it was a nation", I often said to myself. "For is it necessary, is it possible for individual people to be all that interesting?" Not at all! "The question is whether a quantity of talents, powers and capabilities is distributed among the great mass of the people, and whether these talents can be developed through favourable circumstances and first-rate people to a common purpose." I was now pleased to find so little striking originality among my fellow-countrymen; I was pleased that they did not scorn to accept some direction from outside; I was pleased to have found a leader.

'Lothair—let me refer to my friend by his dear Christian name—had always presented the Germans to me from the point of view of their valour and had demonstrated to me that there is no braver nation in the world when they are properly led, and I felt ashamed at never having thought of this first quality of a people. He was familiar with history and he had connections with most men of merit of his time. For all his own youth, he had an eye for the budding, hopeful young people of his country and for the quiet labours of busy and active men in so many fields. He caused me to cast an eye over Germany, what it was and what it could be, and I felt ashamed at having judged a nation by the confused crowd that may press into a theatre cloakroom. He made me consider it my duty to make an impression that was honest, intelligent and stimulating in my speciality too. I now felt myself to be inspired whenever I appeared on the stage. Mediocre passages turned to gold in my mouth, and if a poet had stood by me at that time for appropriate purposes, I should have produced the most wonderful effects.

'Thus the young widow went on to live for some months. He could not do without me, and I was most unhappy when he was away. He showed me the letters of his relations, of his wonderful sister. He showed sympathetic interest in the smallest details of my circumstances; no concord can be thought of as more heartfelt and complete. The word love was not mentioned. He came and went, went and came—and now, my friend, it is high time for you to go too.'

Chapter Seventeen

Wilhelm could not put off visiting his business friends any longer. It was not without embarrassment that he went there; for he knew that he would find letters from his own people there. He was afraid of the reproaches which they would inevitably contain; probably the business-house had also been given news of the embarrassment that was being experienced on his account. After having had so many knightly adventures he shrank from the schoolboyish role in which he would appear, and made up his mind to behave in a really defiant manner, and in this way to conceal his embarrassment.

However, to his great surprise and pleasure it all went very agreeably. In the big, bustling and busy office the people scarcely had time to hunt out his letters; his fairly lengthy absence was only thought of in passing. And when he opened the letters from his father and his friend Werner, he found them all very tolerable in their contents. The old man, in the hope of a detailed diary-account, which he had carefully recommended to his son on parting and for which he had given him a tabular plan to take with him, seemed fairly undisturbed at the silence of the first period, while he complained only of the puzzling nature of the the first and only letter which had been sent off from the Count's residence. Werner only made jokes in his particular way, retailed funny stories of the town and asked for news about friends and acquaintances whom Wilhelm would now meet frequently in the big commercial city. Our friend who was extremely pleased to be getting off so easily, at once replied in some very cheerful letters and promised his father a detailed account of his travels together with all the desired geographical, statistical and mercantile data. He had seen a lot on the journey and hoped to be able to put together a considerable account about it. He did not notice that he was almost in the same position as he had been in when he had lit lights and summoned an audience in order to perform a play which had not been written and even less memorized. When he, therefore, really started to set about his account he became unfortunately aware that he could talk and give an account of emotions and thoughts, and of many experiences of heart and mind, but not of external things to which, as he now noticed, he had not paid the least attention.

In this predicament his friend Laertes' knowledge came to be very useful to him. The two young people, dissimilar as they were, had been linked together by habit, and for all his faults Laertes with his peculiarities was really an interesting person. As he was of a cheerful, happy sensuousness by disposition, he could have grown old without thinking about his condition at all. But his misfortune and sickness had now robbed him of the pure feeling of youth and had revealed to him on the other hand a glimpse of the transient and dismembered quality of our existence. This had led to a moody and rhapsodic way of thinking about things, or rather of expressing direct impressions about them. He did not like being alone, wandered around all the cafés and inns, and if he did stay at home, books on travel were his favourite, indeed his only reading. He could satisfy his wish for reading now, as he had discovered a large lending library, and soon half the world was haunting his good memory.

How easy it was for him to be encouraging to his friend when the latter disclosed to him what a complete lack of material there was to act as basis of the account which he had so solemnly promised. 'Now we can work out a clever scheme which will be quite unique,' Laertes said. 'Is it not the case that Germany has been travelled through, passed through, journeyed through and flown through from one end to the other? And doesn't every German traveller have the magnificent advantage of being able to get his expenses, great or small, refunded by the public? Just tell me the route of your journey before you joined us here; the rest I know. I will look out for you the sources and ancillary material for your work; we must see that there is a supply of square miles that have never been surveyed before and of populations that have not been counted. We can take information about countries' revenues from reference-books and lists which are, as is known, the most reliable documents. We can use these as the support for our political comments; there should be no lack of side-glances at the governments. We can describe a few princes as true fathers of the nation, so that people will be all the more inclined to believe us when we make critical remarks about some of the others; and if we don't actually journey through the places of residence of some famous people, we can meet them in an inn and let them talk the silliest rubbish to us in confidence. In particular let us not forget to work in in the most charming manner a love-story with some naive girl, and the result will be a work that will not only fill father and mother with delight, but which all booksellers too will pay you for with pleasure.'

They set about it, and the two friends had a lot of enjoyment in their work, while in the evenings Wilhelm found very great satisfaction in going to the theatre and in being in the company of Serlo and Aurelia, and every day he could disseminate his ideas further, which had been moving all too long in a narrow circle.

Chapter Eighteen

It was with great interest that he learnt Serlo's life-story piece by piece; for this strange man was not used to being confiding and to talking about anything consecutively. He had been born and nurtured on the stage, one might say. Already as a mute child he could not but move audiences by his mere presence, since even in those days playwrights were familiar with these natural and innocent expedients, and the first time he said 'father' and 'mother' in popular plays he earned himself the greatest applause before he realized what clapping meant. More than once he came down trembling from on high as Amor, made his way out of the egg as Harlequin, and at an early stage performed the neatest tricks as a little chimney-sweep.

Unfortunately he had to pay very dearly in the intervening periods for the applause which he gained on lustrous evenings. His father, convinced that children's attention could only be aroused and held by blows, beat him at regular intervals during the learning of every part; not because the child was clumsy, but so that he would show himself to be all the more certainly and persistently capable. Thus in former times when a boundary-stone was being set up, the children round about had their ears soundly boxed, and very old people still remember exactly where it happened. He grew up and displayed extraordinary capabilities of mind and body, and at the same time a great suppleness, both in his type of imagination and in his actions and gestures. His gift of mimicry exceeded all belief. Even as a boy he could imitate people in such a way that it seemed as if they were visibly there, although they were completely dissimilar from him and each other in figure, age and character. At the same time he was not without the gift of putting up with things, and as soon as he was aware to some extent of his own strength he found nothing more natural than to run away from his father who found it necessary, as the boy's reason and skill increased, to give these qualities support still by severe treatment.

How happy the roguish boy now felt in the free world about him as his pranks ensured him a ready welcome everywhere! His lucky star led him firstly to a monastery during shrovetide where he made an appearance in the guise of a helpful guardian-angel because the father who was responsible for processions and for entertaining the Christian community with sacred masquerades had just died. He also at once took over the part of Gabriel in the Annunciation and made quite an impression on the pretty girl who as Mary very charmingly received the courteous greeting which he extended to her with outward humility and inward pride. After that he played in turn the major part in the mystery plays and thought very well of himself when in the end he was as Saviour mocked by the world, beaten and affixed to the cross.

It may well be that some of the soldiers played their parts only too naturally on this occasion; and so, in order to have his revenge of them in the most apposite way, he put them into the most magnificent clothes of emperors and kings on the occasion of the

Day of Judgment, and at the moment when they were very pleased with their parts and were about to take the step of taking precedence over everybody else in heaven as well, he unexpectedly appeared before them in the shape of the devil and gave them a good hiding with the oven-fork, to the very hearty edification of the whole audience and beggars, and pressed them back mercilessly into the pit where they saw themselves received in the most uncomfortable way by a fire that was emerging from it.

He was astute enough to see that the crowned heads would take umbrage at his cheeky behaviour and would have no respect for his privileged office as accuser and executor of the law; he therefore slipped off quietly before the millenium had yet started, and in a neighbouring town he was received with open arms by a group which was known at that time as Children of Joy. They were understanding, intelligent and lively people, who had the insight that the total of our existence, when divided by reason, never goes out completely, but that there is always a strange fraction as remainder. At certain times they made deliberate efforts to get rid of this fraction which is obstructive and dangerous when dispersed over the whole mass. For one day in each week they behaved as complete jesters and inflicted punishment on each other by means of allegorical performances for the follies they had noticed in themselves and in others during the other days of the week. Even if this method was at the same time cruder as a course of training in which a morally conscious person is accustomed to note, warn and reprimand, none the less it was more amusing and more certain; for although there was a willingness not to deny a certain pet-jester his freedom, he was treated only as what he was, instead of his coming to rule in the house by the other method, with the help of self-deception, and of compelling reason to that secret servitude which is under the illusion of having chased away illusion a long time ago. The fool's mask went around the group, and each one was allowed on his particular day to decorate his mask in an individual way with his own or other people's attributes. They took many liberties during the carnival season and vied with the efforts of the clergy at entertaining and attracting the people. The solemn allegorical processions of virtues and vices, arts and sciences, continents and seasons made a number of concepts tangible to the people and gave them ideas about remote objects, and so these jests were not without use, whereas from another point of view the ecclesiastical mummeries only helped to give further confirmation to a tasteless superstition.

Here too young Serlo was again wholly in his element; he did not have actual inventive powers, but he did possess the greatest skill in using, adapting and making plausible what was available. His ideas, his imitative gifts, even his biting wit, which he was allowed to give free rein, even against his benefactors, at least one day in the week, caused him to be esteemed by the whole group and indeed indispensable to them.

But his restlessness soon drove him away from this advantageous situation into other areas of his country where once more he had to submit to new schooling. He came to that part of Germany which is cultivated but dispenses with pictures and images, and where there is admittedly no lack of truth, though often of intelligence, in the respect for the good and the beautiful; he could not do anything more with his masks; he had to seek to affect heart and emotions. He only remained for short periods with a number of companies, both large and small, and took the opportunity to make note of the peculiarities of all the plays and actors. He soon realized what monotony then ruled on German stages, and was aware of the silly cadences and sounds of Alexandrine verse, as of the stilted and flat dialogue and the dry and platitudinous quality of the directly didactic writers; at the same time he noticed what had an emotional effect and pleased the public.

He found it easy to retain in his memory not *one* part from the current plays, but whole works, together with the particular style of the actor whose performance had been applauded. Then in the course of his ramblings, when he had completely run out of money, he chanced on the idea of giving solo performances of entire plays, particularly in aristocratic houses and in villages, and of thereby procuring at once board and lodging for himself wherever he went. His stage was soon set up in any inn, room or garden; he knew how to capture his audiences' imagination and deceive their senses with a roguish seriousness and an apparent enthusiasm, and before their eyes to convert an old cupboard into a castle and a fan into a dagger. His youthful glow was a substitute for the lack of deep feeling; his vehemence seemed to be strength and his flattery tenderness. He reminded those who were already familiar with the theatre of everything that they had seen and heard, and he aroused in the others an intuitive sense of something wonderful and the wish to know it more closely. If something had an effect in one locality, he did not fail to repeat it somewhere else, and he was most cordially gleeful if he could make fun of everybody in the same way by his extempore acting.

With his lively mind, that was open and in no way inhibited, he very rapidly improved his performance, for he often repeated parts he had learnt and plays. Soon he was speaking and acting in a way that was closer to the meaning than the models whom at first he had merely imitated. In this way he gradually got into the way of acting naturally and yet of always being involved in pretence. He seemed to be carried away and was calculating the effect, and he was above all proud of being able to stir peoples' emotions by degrees. Even the crazy craft itself that he was pursuing soon compelled him to proceed with a certain moderation, and thus he learnt, partly compelled by circumstances and partly from instinct, something that so few actors seem to understand: to be economical in the use of voice and gestures.

By these means he was able to hold the attention even of rough and unfriendly people and to interest them in himself. As he was content everywhere with the board and lodging offered him, and accepted gratefully every present that was handed to him, indeed on a number of occasions refusing money, when in his opinion he already had enough, he was sent away with letters of recommendation to different addresses, and so he wandered for quite a time from one gentleman's residence to another, where he gave and received quite an amount of pleasure and was not without some very agreeable and enjoyable adventures.

With his inward coldness of temperament there was really nobody he could love; with the sharpness of his glance there was nobody he could respect; for he always saw only the outward peculiarities of people and collected them as specimens for his miming collection. At the same time, he felt extremely offended in his egotism if he did not please everybody and was not applauded everywhere. Gradually he had learnt to pay close attention to the gaining of applause, and had so sharpened his mind that he could not help being a flatterer, not only on the stage but also in everyday life. And so his temperament, his talents and his way of life reacted one with the other in such a way that he could see that, without being observed, he had developed into a perfect actor. Indeed, his recitation, declamation and use of gestures rose up to a high degree of truth, freedom and openness on account of an interplay of action and reaction that seemed strange but was quite natural, while in normal life and its social contacts he seemed to become more and more secretive and affected, even distorted and fearful.

Perhaps we shall talk elsewhere about his fortunes and adventures, and at this juncture we will only notice the following points: that in later times, when he was already a successful man in possession of a distinctive reputation and occupying a good, though not firmly established position, he had acquired the habit of showing himself in a subtle way to be a sophist, with a manner that was in part ironical and in part mocking, and thus making almost all serious conversation impossible. He used the approach particularly towards Wilhelm whenever the latter, as often happened, felt inclined to start a conversation on a general, theoretical topic. In spite of this they enjoyed each other's company very much, and their differing ways of thinking ensured a lively interchange of ideas. Wilhelm wanted to develop everything out of the concepts that he had adopted and to see art considered in a coherent context. He wished to set up definite rules, and to determine what was proper, beautiful and good and deserved applause; all in all, he treated everything most seriously. Serlo on the other hand took the matter very lightly; while never answering a question directly, he was able to present the neatest and most entertaining of explanations by means of a story or amusing anecdote, and to entertain the company by enlivening them.

Chapter Nineteen

Now while Wilhelm was spending some very pleasant hours in this way, Melina and the others found themselves in a situation that was all the more tiresome. They often seemed to our friend like evil spirits, and made an irksome impression on him not merely by their presence, but often by their sullen faces and bitter words. Serlo had not even allowed them to have roles as visiting actors, let alone given them any hope of a contract, and yet none the less he had gradually got to know all their capabilities. Whenever actors came to him on a social basis he made a point of getting them to read aloud and often of joining in the reading himself. He chose plays that were due to be put on some time in the future, and those which had not been performed for a long time, and in any case for the most part only partially. Thus after a first performance he had sections repeated in cases where there was some point to be recalled; in this way he increased the actors' insight and strengthened their certainty of achieving the right result. And just as a limited but accurate understanding can effect more to the satisfaction of others than a confused and impure mind of genius, so he raised up mediocre talents to an admirable standard of achievement through the distinct insight that he procured for them imperceptibly. A contributory factor of some importance was that he also had poems read out, and these were discovered to contain the essence of that attraction which well delivered rhythm arouses within us, whereas on other occasions a start was already made in reciting only that prose which was familiar to everybody.

On such occasions also he had got to know all the actors who had recently arrived, had judged what they were and what they might become, and had quietly resolved at once to take advantage of their talents in connection with a revolution that was threatening his company. He let the matter rest for a while and shrugged his shoulders whenever Wilhelm made intercessions on their behalf, until he felt that the right time had come, when he wholly unexpectedly made the suggestion to his young friend that he himself should go on the stage under his direction and that if this condition were accepted he would be willing to take on the others as well.

'These people can't after all be as useless as you have described· them to me hitherto,' Wilhelm replied to him, 'if now they can all be taken on together, and I should have thought that their talents would be the same whether I was there or not.'

Then Serlo revealed the position to him, in strict confidence. The actor who played parts as leading lover was threatening to put up his price when it came to renewing his contract, and Serlo was not inclined to give way to him, especially as he was no longer so popular with the public. If he let this man go, all his supporters would follow him, and in this way the company would lose some good members, but also some mediocre ones. Then he explained to Wilhelm what on the other hand he was hoping to gain from him, Laertes, the Blustering Old Man and even from Madame Melina. Indeed, he promised to see that there would be definite applause even for the poor Pedant in parts as a Jew, a minister of state, or as a villain generally.

Wilhelm was taken aback and heard what was said not without disquiet, and after taking a deep breath he replied, though only in order to say something: 'You talk in a very friendly way only about the good qualities you find in us and hope of us; but what about those weak spots, which certainly won't have escaped your sharp eyes?'

'By putting in some hard work, rehearsals and thought we shall soon change weakness into strength,' Serlo rejoined. 'There's nobody amongst you all, even if you are only naturalist actors and bunglers, who could not be said to offer a certain amount of hope, more or less; for as far as I can judge, there isn't anybody in the group whom I would call a stick, and it's only the sticks you can do nothing about, whether it is their clumsiness and stiffness are due to vanity, stupidity or hypochondria.'

Then Serlo outlined in a few words the terms that he was willing and able to offer; he asked Wilhelm to make up his mind as quickly as possible, and left him in no slight agitation.

In the process of the strange venture of the fictitious travel account which he and Laertes were putting together and which had, as it were, only been undertaken as a joke, Wilhelm had come to take more notice than he usually did of the circumstances and daily life in the real world. It was now for the first time that he came to understand his father's purpose when the latter had so eagerly recommended him to write a journal. He felt for the first time how pleasant and useful it could be to make oneself the focal point of so many trades and needs, and to help spread life and activity right into the most remote mountains and forests of the continent. The lively trading city where he was at present provided him with a most tangible conception of a great centre, in particular in conjunction with the restlessness of Laertes, who dragged him around everywhere; it was a centre from which everything flows out and to which everything returns, and it was the first time that his spirit took real pleasure in the observation of this kind of activity. It was when he was in this position that Serlo had made him the offer and had rekindled his inclinations, his confidence in innate ability and his obligation towards the helpless company.

'Here I stand once more,' he said to himself, 'at the cross-roads between the two ladies who appeared to me in my youth. The one does not look so wretched as she did at that earlier time, and the other looks less splendid. You feel a kind of inner calling to follow the one and the other, and the outward inducements are strong enough; you feel that it is impossible to come to a decision; you would like your vote to be determined by a majority from outside, and yet when you make a thorough search, you find that it is only outward circumstances which imbue you with an inclination to trade, business and ownership, and at the same time that your innermost need induces and encourages the wish to develop and train the proclivities to goodness and beauty within yourself, whether these features are bodily or spiritual. And must I not praise fate that leads me here, without intervention from myself, to the goal of all my wishes? Is not everything which I thought out and resolved previously now happening by chance without my intervention? It is indeed strange! Man appears to have confidence in nothing more than his hopes and aspirations, which he nurtures and cherishes for a long time in his heart; and yet, when they do come his way and, as it were, force themselves upon him, he does not recognize them and retreats from them. Everything that I happened to dream about before that unhappy night which separated me from Mariane stands before me and offers itself to me. It was to this place that I wanted to escape, and I have been gently led here; I wanted to try and find a post with Serlo, and now he is looking for me and offering me conditions which as a beginner I could not expect. For was it only love for Mariane which bound me to the theatre? Or was it love of art that linked me with the girl? Was the prospect of a career on the stage, that way out to the theatre, merely a pretext that would be welcome to an untidy, and restless person who wanted to continue with a way of life that the circumstances of the middle-class world did not permit him, or was everything different, purer, and more dignified? And what was to impel you to change your earlier opinions? Have you not rather been following your plan, though in ignorance yourself, up to now? And is not the final step to be approved still more, as no secondary aims are involved, and as you can both keep a solemn promise and at the same time free yourself in a noble-spirited way from a serious debt of guilt?'

All things stirring in his heart and imagination now alternated and contrasted with one another in the most lively manner. The facts that he could keep his Mignon and that he did not need to repudiate the Harpist were no light weight on the scale, and yet he was still fluctuating this way and that when he went to visit his friend Aurelia in the usual way.

Chapter Twenty

He found her on the couch; she seemed quiet. 'Do you still believe you will be able to go on tomorrow?' he asked. 'Oh yes!' she replied vivaciously. 'You know, nothing will stop me doing that.—If only you knew a way of deflecting away from myself the applause of our audience in the pit: they mean well, but they will kill me yet. The day before yesterday I thought my heart would break! I used to be able to put up with it, certainly, when I was pleased with my own performance; if I had studied and prepared for a long time in advance, I was pleased when the welcome sound indicating that success had been achieved re-echoed from all sides. But now I don't say what I want, nor how I want it; I get carried along, I'm confused, and my acting makes a much greater impression. The applause gets louder, and I think: "If you only knew what it is that enchants you! The dark, intense and ambiguous harmonies move your hearts and compel your admiration, and you do not feel that what you have given your recommendation are the cries of grief of this unhappy woman."

'This morning I was learning my part, just now I have been rehearsing. I am tired and in a state of collapse, and tomorrow we start again from the beginning. There's to be a performance tomorrow evening. And so I drag myself around, this way and that; I find it boring to get up and annoying to go to bed. Everything goes round in a perpetual circle inside me. And then the wretched attempts at consolation appear before me, then I throw them away and curse them. I won't give in, I won't give in to inevitability—why should something be necessary that destroys me? Couldn't it be different as well? I just have to pay for the fact that I am a German; it is the character of Germans to be heavy about everything and for everything to be heavy about them.'

'Oh, my friend,' Wilhelm interposed, 'if only you could stop sharpening the dagger with which you are continually wounding yourself! Are you really left with nothing? Are your youth, your figure, your health, and your talents nothing? If without it being your fault you have lost something of value, must you throw everything else away into the bargain? Is that also inevitable?'

She was silent for a few moments, and then she flared up: 'I know that it's a waste of time, love is nothing but a waste of time! What could I not have accomplished, what ought I not to have done! Now it has all come to nothing. I'm a poor creature that has fallen in love, I'm completely infatuated! Take pity on me, for God's sake, I'm a poor creature!'

She became absorbed in her own thoughts, and after a short interval she cried our fervently: 'You men are used to everybody throwing themselves at you. No, you can't appreciate it, no man is capable of appreciating the value of a woman who has self-respect! By all holy angels, by all the images of bliss which a pure, kind heart conjures up, there is nothing more heavenly than a woman who gives herself to the man she loves. We are cold, proud, sublime, pure and clever, if we deserve to be called women; and we lay down all these virtues at your feet, as soon as we love and as soon as we hope for this love to be requited. Oh, I have thrown away my whole life, consciously and intentionally! But now I too will despair, deliberately despair. Let there be no drop of blood within me that does not receive punishment, no fibre of my being that I am not prepared to torment. Just smile, just laugh at the theatrical display of passion!'

Our friend felt far from any impulse to laughter. Aurelia's dreadful position, half due to nature and half to circumstances, tormented him all too much. He felt with her the anguish of her unhappy tension; his mind was thrown into confusion, and his blood was coursing feverishly.

She had stood up, and was walking up and down in the room. 'I tell myself all the reasons why I should not love him,' she exclaimed. 'I know also that he is not worth it; I turn my emotions away from him, this way and that, and keep myself busy as well as I can. Occasionally I take on the learning of a part, even if I do not have to play it; I rehearse the old roles, which I know by heart, ever more consciously and in detail, and just go on rehearsing—my friend, my confidant, what a terrible piece of work it is to separate oneself forcibly from oneself. My reason is suffering, my brain is under such a strain; in order to save myself from going mad, I abandon myself again to the feeling that I love him.—Yes, I love him, I love him!' she cried out amid a thousand tears, 'I love him, and therefore I am willing to die.'

He grasped her by the hand and implored her not to wear herself out. 'Oh, how strange it is,' he said, 'that man is unable to realize not only much that is impossible, but also much that is possible. You have not been destined to find a faithful heart that would have become your entire happiness. I was destined to attach the whole salvation of my life to an unfortunate woman whom I drew down to the ground like a reed with the heavy weight of my fidelity, and perhaps I even shattered her.'

He had confided to Aurelia the story of his relationship with Mariane, and could therefore make reference to it now. She looked at him fixedly and asked: 'Can you say that you have never yet deceived a woman, that you have not tried to win her favour with frivolous gallantry, with criminal protestations or with seductive vows?'

'That I can,' replied Wilhelm, 'and indeed, without boasting; for my life has been very simple, and I have seldom been tempted to be a tempter. And my beautiful and noble friend, what a warning to me is the sad condition in which I see you! Receive a vow from me that is wholly fitting to my heart's state, which expresses itself in my case in language and form by means of the emotion which you have caused me to feel and which this moment makes sacred. I will resist all transient inclinations, and even the most serious ones I will keep locked within my heart; no woman shall hear a confession of love from my lips unless I can dedicate my whole life to her!'

She looked at him with a glance of wild indifference and went several steps back when he held out his hand to her. 'It's of no consequence!' she cried; 'so many women's tears more or less won't make the sea-level rise. But,' she continued, 'to save one woman among thousands is something all the same, and it is acceptable to find one honest man among thousands! Do you know also what it is you are promising?'

'I do know,' Wilhelm rejoined with a smile, stretching out his hand.

'I accept it,' she replied, and made a movement with her right hand which led him to believe that she would take hold of his hand; but she rapidly opened her bag, took out the dagger as quick as lightning and swiftly went over his hand with the point and the cutting edge. He drew back his hand with speed, but already blood was running down.

'You men must be given a sharp warning, if you are to be made to pay attention!' she cried and with a fierce cheerfulness which soon turned into hasty activity. She took her handkerchief and bound his hand with it, to staunch the first flow of blood. 'Forgive a woman who is half crazy,' she exclaimed, 'and don't regret these drops of blood. I am reconciled, I am myself again. I will go down on my knees to apologize; do let me have the consolation of healing you.'

She hurried to her cupboard, fetched linen and other things, staunched the blood and inspected the wound carefully. The cut went through the ball just below the thumb, divided the life-line and came to an end by the little finger. She bandaged it quietly and seemed turned in upon herself with a thoughtful significance. He asked a number of times: 'My dear, how could you do harm to your friend?'

'Quiet!,' she replied, laying her finger on her lips, 'Quiet!'

BOOK FIVE

Chapter One

In this way Wilhelm acquired over and above his two scarcely healed wounds a fresh, third injury which caused him not a little discomfort. Aurelia would not admit that he needed professional help; she herself bound his wound amid all kinds of strange speeches, ceremonies and sayings, and put him into a very embarrassing situation by all this. Yet not he alone, but everyone who happened to be near her, suffered from her restlessness and eccentricity, though no more than little Felix. The lively child was most impatient as a result of such pressures, and he behaved all the worse, the more she reprimanded and corrected him.

The boy indulged in certain peculiarities, which are also usually referred to as naughtiness, and which she was by no means inclined to condone in him. For instance, he preferred to drink out of a bottle rather than a glass, and evidently he found food tastier in a dish than on a plate. Such unseemliness was not overlooked, and if he now left a door open or banged it to and, after being given an order, he either did not budge from the spot or else rushed obstreperously away, he had to listen to a long lecture, though without showing any improvement in his behaviour afterwards. On the contrary, his liking for Aurelia seemed to dwindle daily; there was nothing affectionate in his voice when he called her mother, in fact he was passionately attached to the old nurse who, it was true, let him do what he liked.

But for some time she too had become so ill that she had to be taken away from the house to some quiet accommodation, and Felix would have been entirely on his own, if Mignon had not appeared as a kindly protective spirit to him as well. Both children kept each other entertained in the most delightful way; she taught him little songs, and he, having a very good memory, often recited them, to the astonishment of his listeners. She also tried to explain to him the maps which she still concerned herself with, though in doing so she did not make use of the best method. For actually she did not seem to have any special interest in the different countries apart from whether they were cold or warm. She could give a very good account of the polar regions, of the terrible ice there, and of the increasing warmth the further away one went from them. When anyone was going on a journey, her only question was whether he was going north or south, and she made efforts to find the way on her little maps. In particular, whenever Wilhelm talked about travelling she was very attentive and always seemed to be cast down as soon as the conversation turned to other topics. Though she could not be persuaded to play a part or even to visit the theatre during a performance, she learnt odes and songs by heart gladly and industriously, and aroused everyone's surprise whenever she declaimed, often in an unexpected and impromptu manner, this type of poem which was usually a work of the serious and solemn sort.

Serlo, habitually on the look-out for all traces of budding talent, tried to encourage her; for the most part, however, she recommended herself to him by her very agreeable, varied and sometimes even cheerful singing, and it was in just this way that the Harpist had won his favour.

Without having an outstanding gift for music or being able to play any instrument, Serlo was able to appreciate the high value of this art; he tried as often as he could to procure for himself this pleasure, which can be compared to no other. Once a week he held a concert, and now through Mignon, the Harpist and Laertes, who was not unskilled with the violin, a strange little private orchestra had been formed.

He was fond of saying: 'Man is so inclined to concern himself with the most ordinary things, while his mind and senses are so easily blunted against impressions of beauty and perfection, that we should use all means to preserve the capacity of feeling them. For nobody can entirely do without such a pleasure, and it is only because they are not used to enjoying anything good that a lot of people are prepared to find enjoyment in what is silly and in bad taste, so long as it is new. Each day,' he said, 'we should at least hear one little song, read one good poem, see one first-rate picture and, if it can be arranged, utter some sensible remarks.'

With these opinions, which so to speak came naturally to Serlo, there could be no lack of agreeable entertainment for those in his circle. In the midst of these pleasurable circumstances Wilhelm one day received a letter with black sealing-wax. Werner's seal was an indication of sad news, and Wilhelm was not a little shocked when he found the death of his father announced just in a few phrases. He had departed from the world after a short and unexpected illness, and had left his domestic affairs in best order.

This unexpected news affected Wilhelm to the core of his being. He felt deeply with what insensitivity we often neglect friends and relations as long as they are enjoying with us their earthly sojourn, and how we only regret the omission when the lovely relationship has been terminated, at least for now. What is more, grief at the early death of the worthy man could only be tempered by the feeling that there was little in the world that he had loved and by the conviction that there was little he had enjoyed.

Wilhelm's thoughts soon turned to his own circumstances, and he felt not a little disturbed. No one can be put into a more dangerous situation than when a great change in his position is effected through outward circumstances without his ways of feeling and thinking having been prepared for it. Then an epoch which is no epoch ensues, and a contradiction comes into being which is all the more marked, the less the person involved notices that he is not yet prepared for the new circumstances.

Wilhelm found himself free at a time in which he could not yet be clear in his own mind. His opinions were noble, his purposes pure, and his plans did not seem reprehensible. All this he could concede to himself with some confidence; but he had had sufficient opportunity to notice that he lacked experience, and for that reason he placed an excessive value on the experiences of others and on the consequences which they derived from them with conviction, and because of this he only went even further astray. He believed that he could acquire what he lacked in the first place if he attempted to retain and collect everything memorable that he might encounter in books and conversation. He therefore wrote down the opinions and ideas of others as well as of himself, indeed whole conversations which interested him, and in this way unfortunately held on to what was false as well as what was true, clinging far too long to one idea, indeed, it might be said, to one maxim, and in the process he moved away from his natural manner of thinking and acting, as he often followed alien lights as his guiding-stars. Aurelia's bitterness and his friend Laertes's cold contempt for mankind prejudiced his judgment more frequently than was reasonable: but nobody had been more dangerous to him than Jarno, a man whose clear understanding of immediate matters passed fair, severe judgment, but at the same time made the mistake of uttering these individual judgments with a kind of general validity, whereas the dicta of the understanding in fact are only valid once, and what is more in their own most specific instances, and already become false when they are applied to the next case.

Thus Wilhelm became even further separated from wholesome unity, even while he was striving to become one with himself, and with this confusion his passions found it all the easier to make use of all preparations for their own advantage, and only to make him all the more confused about what he had to do.

Serlo used the news of the death to his own advantage, and what is more he really had every day more cause to be thinking of a new structure to his company. He either had to renew old contracts, for which he had no great inclination, as a number of the members of the company who believed themselves to be indispensable daily became more intolerable; or else he would have to give the company a completely new shape, and this also tallied with his own wishes.

Without pressing Wilhelm himself, he aroused tensions in Aurelia and Philine; and the rest of the company, who were longing to be taken on, likewise left no peace for our friend, so that he found himself standing in some embarrassment at a crossroads. Who would have thought that a letter from Werner, which had been written entirely in the contrary sense, would finally press him into a decision? We will leave out only the preliminary material, and otherwise we will reproduce the letter with few changes.

Chapter Two

'Thus it was right, as indeed it really has to be, for everyone to pursue their calling and show their activity on each occasion that is possible. The worthy old man had scarcely died when already in the following quarter of an hour nothing in the house was happening as he would have liked it. Friends, acquaintances and relatives pressed round, but in particular all types of humanity of the sort that have something to gain on such occasions. People brought and carried, paid, wrote and reckoned; some fetched wine and cakes, others drank and ate; but I saw nobody more seriously occupied than the women, while they were seeking mourning clothes.

'You will, therefore, pardon me, my dear fellow if I thought also of *my* advantage on this occasion, if I showed myself as helpful and as active as possible with regard to your sister, and if I made it clear to her, as soon as it was reasonably proper, that it was now up to us to hasten the advent of a union, which up to now our fathers had delayed because of their excessive formality.

'Now you must not think that we have had the idea of taking possession of the big empty house. We are more modest and more

sensible; you shall hear our plan. After the wedding your sister is
to move straightaway into our house, and in fact your mother as
well.

'Now you must not think that we have had the idea of taking
for yourselves in the place.'' That is just the art, my friend! Clever
management makes everything possible, and you wouldn't believe
how much space you can find when you don't need a lot of room.
We are selling the big house, and there is a good opportunity to do
this right away; the money resulting from the sale is to bear
interest a hundredfold.

'I hope you will agree with this, and trust that you have not
inherited any of the sterile hobbies of your father and
grandfather. The latter placed his greatest happiness in a number
of insignificant works of art which nobody, I may indeed say
nobody, could enjoy with him: the former lived in expensively
appointed accommodation which he did not let anyone enjoy with
him. We wish to do things differently, and I hope for your
agreement.

'It is true, I myself retain in our whole house no place except
that at my desk, and as yet I can't foresee where at some future
date a cradle is to be put; but to make up for this, there is all the
more space outside the house. Cafés and clubs for the husband,
walks and rides for the wife, and beautiful places of entertainment
in the country for both of us. At the same time the greatest
advantage is that our round table is fully occupied and that it will
be impossible for father to see friends who only find faults with
him the more flippantly, the more trouble he has taken to be
hospitable to them.

'Let us have nothing superfluous in the house! Let us not have
too much furniture or too many implements, let us do without
coach and horses! Nothing but money, and then you can do what
you like every day in a sensible manner. Let us have no wardrobe,
but the newest and best of clothes on our persons; the husband
can wear his coat until it is worn out, and the wife can sell off hers
as soon as it is somewhat out of fashion. I find nothing more
unbearable than a lot of old lumber. If I were to be presented with
the most costly jewel on condition that I wore it daily on my
finger, I would not accept it; for however can we conceive of any
happiness in the case of dead capital? This then is my merry
confession of faith: to do business, make money, amuse yourself
with your own people and have no further care for the rest of the
world, except in so far as you can make use of it.

'But now you will say: "What thought is there for *me* in your
pretty plan? Where am I to be fitted in if you sell my paternal
home and there is not the slightest room left in yours?"'

'Certainly this is the main point, my little brother, and I shall
be able to oblige you in this respect immediately, as soon as I have
expressed appropriate appreciation of the excellent way you have
been using your time.

'Just tell me, how did you set about becoming a connoisseur of
all sorts of useful and interesting things in such a short time?
Capable though I know you to be, I still would not have credited
you with such attentiveness and industry. Your diary has
convinced us how useful the journey has been to you; the
description of the iron-headed hammers and the copper hammers
is excellent and indicates much insight into the matter. I visited
these too at an earlier time; but my account, when I compare it
with yours, looks very clumsy. The whole of the letter about linen
manufacture is instructive, and the note about the competition is
very telling. Occasionally you make arithmetical mistakes, but
these are very pardonable.

'But what pleases my father and myself mostly and above all
are your thorough soundly based judgments on the management
and especially on the improvement of country estates. We are
hoping to buy up a big estate that has been sequestrated and
which is in a very fertile area. We can use for this purpose the
money to be made from the paternal home; some can be lent, and
some can remain; and we are counting on your going there to be
in charge of the improvements, and in this way the estate can
increase in value by a third in a few years, and this is not too high
a claim; then it can be sold, a bigger one can be sought for,
renovated and put on the market again, and you are the man for
this. In the meantime our pens at home shall not be idle, and we
shall soon place ourselves in enviable circumstances.

'Now farewell! Enjoy life on your travels and go wherever you
find things pleasurable and useful. We shan't need you for six
months; you can, therefore, look around the world as you please:
for a clever man obtains the best education in travelling. Farewell,
I am pleased to be so closely linked with you, and also now to be
united with you in the spirit of activity.'

However well this letter was written and however many
economic truths it might contain, it displeased Wilhelm for a
number of reasons none the less. The praise he had received for
his feigned statistical, technical and agricultural knowledge was a
silent reproach to him; and the ideal which his brother-in-law
sketched out for him concerning the happiness of middle-class life
did not attract him at all; rather, a secret spirit of contradiction
drove him impetuously to the opposing extreme. He convinced
himself that it was only in the theatre that he could complete the

form of education that he wanted to give himself, and he seemed
to be becoming all the more strengthened in his resolution, the
more vigorously Werner had become, without realizing it, his
opponent. With this he marshalled all his arguments, and
confirmed himself in his own opinion all the more definitely, the
more he believed that he had reason to present his point of view to
the shrewd Werner in a favourable light, and it was in this way
that a reply took shape which we will likewise insert.

Chapter Three

'Your letter is so well written, and so cleverly and ably thought
out that there is nothing more to be added to it. You will pardon
me, however, if I say that it is possible to think, assert and act on
the very opposite of what your letter recommends and in spite of
this be right as well. Your way of life and thought looks towards
unrestricted acquisition and a little, cheerful type of pleasure, and
I hardly need to tell you that I can find nothing that would attract
me about it.

'In the first place I have to confess to you unfortunately that my
journal was put together from several books with the help of a
friend as an emergency, in order to please my father, and that I do
know the things contained in it and various further material of
the same kind, but do not understand them at all nor have any
wish to be involved with them. What help is it to me to be
manufacturing good iron, if my own inner being is full of slag?
And what use is it to put a landed estate into order if I am at odds
with myself?

'To put it to you in a few words, it was my wish and intention in
a vague way from childhood onwards to develop and educate
myself, entirely as I am. I still cherish these very views, it is only
that the means which will make this possible for me are rather
clearer to me. I have seen more of the world than you believe, and
made better use of it than you think. Do therefore pay some
attention to what I say, even if it should not be entirely in line
with your way of thinking.

'If I were a nobleman, our disagreement would soon be settled;
but as I am only from the middle classes, I must take a path of my
own, and I trust that you will understand me. I don't know how it
is in other countries, but in Germany it is only the nobleman who
has the possibility of a certain general and, if I may say so,

personal development. Someone from the middle classes can acquire merit and, if need be, educate his mind; but as far as his personality is concerned, he is lost, whatever approach he takes. A nobleman, who mixes with the most distinguished people, takes it as his duty to display a refined demeanour, and this demeanour becomes an open propriety, since no doors are closed to him, and since he has to pay with his figure and person, whether at court or in the army: consequently he has reason to make something of his figure and person, and to show that he does. A certain solemn gracefulness while dealing with ordinary things and a kind of frivolous elegance in the case of serious and important matters suit him well because he can disclose that he retains his balance on all occasions. He is a public personage, and the more cultivated his movements are, the more sonorous his voice, and the more restrained and measured his whole character is, the more perfect he is. If he is always the same in his attitude to high and low, to friends and relations, there is nothing to criticize about him, it is not right to wish him to be different. Let him be cold, but understanding; dissimulating, but shrewd. If he can control himself outwardly at every moment of his life, nobody has any further claim to make on him, and everything that he has within and around himself, capability, talent, riches, all these seem to be only extras.

'Now imagine to yourself any middle-class person who might be thinking of making only a limited number of claims on those advantages; he cannot but fail completely, and he would have to become all the unhappier, the more his own nature had given him the capability and drive for that kind of life.

'If a nobleman knows no frontiers in ordinary life, if kings or king-like figures can be made from him, he may appear everywhere with a quiet consciousness of being with his own sort; he may press forward in all cases, whereas nothing befits middle-class man better than the clear quiet awareness of the boundary line that has been drawn about him. He may not ask: "What are you?" but only: "What do you have? What insight, what knowledge, what ability, how much wealth?" If the nobleman gives everything through the presentation of his person, the man from the middle classes gives nothing by means of his personality, and is not intended to give anything. The former is allowed to and is supposed to appear; the latter is intended only to be, and what he wishes to appear as is ridiculous and tasteless. The former is to do and act, the latter to produce and provide; he is to develop individual capabilities in order to become useful, and it is assumed already that there is no harmony in his nature, nor need there be any, because he must neglect everything else in order to make himself useful in one particular way.

'It is not for instance the arrogance of the nobles and the subservience of the middle classes that are responsible for this difference, but the structure of society itself; whether one day it can be changed at all, and what is going to be changed, are of little concern to me; enough, the way things are at present, I have to think of myself, and how I can save myself and achieve what to me is an indispensable need.

'Now I do happen to have an irresistible yearning for precisely that harmonious development of my nature which birth denies to me. Since leaving you, I have gained a lot through physical exercise; I have laid aside much of my habitual shyness and present myself in a fairly tolerable manner. Likewise I have trained my speech and voice, and I may say without vanity that I do not make a bad impression in social gatherings. Now I don't deny that my urge to be a public figure and to win approval and to make an impact in a wider circle grows daily more insuperable. Added to that is my liking for literature and for everything that is connected with it, and the need to cultivate my mind and my taste, so that gradually, even in the case of the pleasure that I cannot do without, I shall judge only what is good really as good and what is beautiful as beautiful. You can see indeed that all this, as far as I am concerned, is only to be found in the theatre, and that it is only in this one element that I can be active and fulfil myself as I would like. On the stage an educated man appears as well personally in his lustre as in the upper classes; mind and body have to keep in step with every effort made, and I shall be able to be and to appear there as well as anywhere else. If I want further occupation as well, there is plenty of mechanical drudgery there, and I can procure daily practice in patience.

'Do not argue with me about it; for the step will already have been taken before you can write to me. I intend to change my name because of the current prejudices and because in any case I am ashamed to appear with the name Meister. Farewell. Our possessions are in such good hands that I have no worry about them at all; I shall ask you from time to time for what I need; it will not be much, for I hope that my art will also keep me.'

The letter had scarcely been sent off when Wilhelm at once kept his word and declared his position right away, to the astonishment of Serlo and the others: he would devote himself to the acting profession and was willing to enter into a contract on reasonable terms. Agreement about these was soon reached, for already at an earlier stage Serlo had put forward proposals in such a way that

Wilhelm and the others could be well pleased. All members of the stranded troupe, with whom we have been concerned for so long, were at once accepted, though without anyone, except perhaps Laertes, showing any gratitude to Wilhelm. Just as they had made their demands without any sense of trust, so they were thankless in receiving. Most of them preferred to ascribe their appointment to the influence of Philine and addressed their expressions of gratitude to her. In the meantime the contracts that had been prepared were signed, and through an inexplicable association of ideas the image of that wooded setting where he had been wounded and had been lying in Philine's lap arose before Wilhelm's imagination at the moment when he was signing his fictitious name. The delightful Amazon came out of the bushes on a white horse, approached him and dismounted. Her helpful and friendly endeavours bade her come and go; at last she stood before him. The garment fell from her shoulders; her face and figure began to gleam, and she disappeared. So he only affixed his name automatically, without knowing what he was doing, and it was not until he had signed that he was aware that Mignon was standing by his side, holding him by the arm, and that she had been trying to pull his hand away.

Chapter Four

One of the conditions on which Wilhelm was willing to take up the theatrical profession had not been conceded unreservedly by Serlo. The former insisted that *Hamlet* should be performed in its entirety without cuts, and the latter was prepared to put up with the strange desire, provided that it should be 'possible'. Now they had had many an argument about this earlier; for both had very different opinions about what was or was not possible, and about what could be left out of the play without dismembering it.

Wilhelm was still in that happy period when we cannot understand that there can be anything lacking about a girl whom we love or about an author we admire. Our feeling for them is so complete and undivided that we are compelled to think that they too embody an equally perfect harmony. Serlo on the other hand liked to differentiate, and did so almost too much; his sharp mind was usually willing to recognize in a work of art only a more or less incomplete whole. He believed that there was little reason for treating plays with circumspection, seeing what they were like, and so Shakespeare, and in particular *Hamlet*, had to put up with a lot.

Wilhelm did not want to listen when Serlo talked about separating the wheat from the chaff. 'It isn't a mixture of wheat and chaff,' Wilhelm exclaimed, 'it is one trunk, with branches, leaves, buds, blossom and fruit. Is not the one created with and through the other?' Serlo contended that there was no need to put the whole trunk on to the table; the artist should offer his guests apples of gold in pictures of silver. They wore themselves out with figures of speech, and their views seemed increasingly to diverge.

Our friend felt quite close to despair when on one occasion after a long argument Serlo advised him to take the simplest step, to make up his mind there and then, to pick up his pen, to cut from the tragedy whatever would not or could not be fitted in, and to compress several characters into one, and if he was not as yet sufficiently familiar with this approach or did not as yet have the heart for it, he should leave the job to him, and he would soon have it finished.

'That's not according to our agreement,' Wilhelm replied. 'How can you have so much good taste and yet be so frivolous?'

'My friend,' Serlo exclaimed, 'you too will be like that soon. I realize only too well the repugnant aspect of this manner which has not as yet perhaps been shown on any stage in the world. But where is there a theatrical practice which is so uncared-for as ours? The authors compel us to this wretched mutilation, and the public allows it. How many plays do we have then that do not go beyond the limits of the personnel, the scenery, the mechanics of the stage, of the time, the dialogue and the physical strength of the actors? And yet we are expected to put on performances, to keep on putting them on, and to keep on putting them on anew. Should we not think of our own interest in the matter, as we can have just as much effect with works that have been hacked about as with those that are given in their entirety? After all, it is the audiences that put us in an advantageous position! There are few Germans, and perhaps only a few people from all the nations of today, who have feeling for an aesthetic whole; they only praise and blame in a partial way; their raptures are only of a partial kind: and for whom is that more fortunate than for the actors, since the theatre always remains only as a patched and cobbled thing.'

'It may well be,' Wilhelm rejoined, 'but does it have to remain so, does everything have to remain the way it is? Don't convince me that you are right; for no power on earth would be able to persuade me to keep to a contract which I had only agreed to through the crudest of mistakes.'

Serlo brought a light note into the discussion and asked Wilhelm to think again about their frequent conversations on *Hamlet* and to work out for himself the ways and means of providing a felicitous adaptation.

After a few days spent in isolation, Wilhelm returned with a cheerful countenance. 'I would be very much mistaken,' he exclaimed, 'if I haven't found a method of dealing with the whole; indeed I am convinced that Shakespeare would have done it himself like this if his genius had not been directed so much to the main aim and had not been led astray by the novellas that he was working from.'

'Let's hear what you've got to say,' said Serlo, as he sat down ceremoniously on the sofa; 'I shall listen quietly, but at the same time I shall judge all the more severely.'

Wilhelm went on: 'I am not afraid; just you listen. After the most searching investigation and the most mature consideration I distinguish two elements in the structure of this play: the first consists of the great inner relationships of the personages and events, the powerful effects which arise out of the characters and actions of the main figures, and these are individually excellent and the sequence in which they are presented cannot be bettered. No kind of treatment can destroy them, and it can scarcely disfigure them. It is they that everyone demands to see, that nobody dares to touch, that make a deep impression on the spirit, and that have almost all, as I hear, been presented on the German stage. Only it is my belief that a mistake has been made in that the second element that is to be noticed in connection with this play, I mean the external relationships of the characters by which they are transported from one place to another or are linked in one way or another through certain events, has been considered to be all too insignificant, has only been talked about in passing or indeed has been left aside. It is true that these threads are only thin and loose, but they do go through the whole play, and hold together what would otherwise fall apart, what also really does fall apart if the threads are cut away, and someone believes that he has gone out of his way to do a favour if he leaves the ends standing.

'Among these external factors I count the disturbances in Norway, the war with young Fortinbras, the embassy to the old uncle, the quarrel that is settled, the expedition of young Fortinbras to Poland and his return at the end; likewise Horatio's return from Wittenberg, Hamlet's wish to go there, the journey of Laertes to France, his return, the despatching of Hamlet to England, his being taken prisoner by the pirates, the death of the two courtiers because of the treacherous letter; all these are circumstances and happenings which can add substance to a novel but which are most harmful to the dramatic unity of this play, in which the hero in particular has no plans, and they are highly incorrect.'

'I'm glad to hear you talking like that for once in a way!' Serlo cried.

'Don't interrupt me,' Wilhelm rejoined, 'You might not always want to praise me. These mistakes are like temporary supports to a building which may not be removed until a firm wall has been set up. So my suggestion is not to lay hand on those great, opening situations, but to be sparing of them as much as possible, both in general and in individual cases, but then suddenly to throw aside all these external, individual, scattered and distracting motivating forces and to substitute in their place one single factor.'

'And what might that be?' Serlo asked, raising himself from his settled position.

'It's already in the play,' Wilhelm replied, 'it's only that I make the right use of it. It's the disturbances in Norway. Here you have my plan if you want to examine it.

'After the death of old Hamlet the Norwegians who were first to be conquered become restless. The governor there sends Horatio, an old school-friend of Hamlet who, however, has excelled all the others in bravery and common sense, to Denmark, in order to press for the arming of the fleet, something which is being started only in a dilatory way under the new king who is devoted only to revelry. Horatio knows the old king, for he has taken part in his last battles and has been favoured by him, and the first scene with the Ghost won't lose anything through it. The new king then gives Horatio an audience and sends Laertes to Norway with the news that the fleet will soon be landing, while Horatio receives the order to hurry up the arming of the fleet; on the other hand his mother is not willing to permit Hamlet to go to sea with Horatio, as he would like to do.'

'Thank God!' Serlo cried, 'in this way we shall be rid of Wittenberg too and the university, which was always a wretched nuisance, as far as I was concerned. I find your idea really attractive; for apart from the two single remote images of Norway and the fleet the audience don't need to *think* about anything; they *see* everything else, it all happens, instead of their imaginations being chased around the whole world, as would otherwise be the case.'

'You will easily see how I can now hold the rest together too,' Wilhelm added. 'When Hamlet reveals to Horatio his stepfather's misdeed, Horatio advises him to go with him to Norway, make sure of the army and return armed. As Hamlet is getting too dangerous for the King and Queen, they have no more convenient way of getting rid of him than to send him after the fleet and to give him Rosencrantz and Guildenstern as observers; and as Laertes comes back in the meantime, this youth, who has been worked up until he is ready to be an assassin, is sent on after him. The fleet is immobile because of unfavourable winds; Hamlet returns once again; his appearance in the churchyard can perhaps be provided with some felicitous motivation; his encounter with Laertes in Ophelia's grave is a great and indispensable moment. At this point the King may consider that it would be better to get rid of Hamlet on the spot; the festival of leave-taking and of the apparent reconciliation with Laertes is now solemnly celebrated, and here tournaments are held, and Hamlet and Laertes fence with one another too. I can't bring the play to a close without the four corpses; nobody is to be left over. As the electoral rights of the people now become valid again, Hamlet expresses his support, as he lies dying, for Horatio.'

'Just be quick about it,' Serlo added, 'sit down and work out the play in detail; the idea has my full approval; we must make sure that the mood of enthusiasm is not lost.'

Chapter Five

For a long time now Wilhelm had been occupied with a translation of *Hamlet*; for this purpose he had made use of the intelligent work of Wieland[1], by means of which he had got to know Shakespeare in the first place. What had been left out in this version, he now added, and so he was in possession of a complete copy at the moment when he had come to a fair measure of agreement with Serlo about the method of approach. He now started to make cuts and insertions, to separate and to link up, to change and often to restore, according to his own plan; for, contented as he was with his own idea, it none the less seemed to him when he was putting it into practice that it only meant that the original was being spoilt.

1. Christoph Martin Wieland's German prose translation of twenty-two Shakespeare plays appeared in eight volumes between 1762 and 1766. (Tr.)

As soon as he was ready, he read it aloud to Serlo and the rest of the troupe. They declared themselves very satisfied with it; Serlo especially made a great number of complimentary observations.

'You have very rightly felt that this play is accompanied by external circumstances,' he said among other things, 'but that these must be simpler than the way they have been presented to us by the great poet. What happens off-stage, what the audience does not see and has to imagine, is like a background in front of which the acting figures move. The big, simple prospect looking toward the fleet and Norway will be very helpful to the play; if this were to be entirely removed, the play would only be a family scene, and the great conception that here a whole royal house is collapsing through inner crimes and ineptitude would not be delineated in its whole dignity. But if that background itself were to remain multifarious, mobile and confused, it would be damaging to the impression of the characters.'

Now Wilhelm came to the defence of Shakespeare again and demonstrated that he had been writing for island-dwellers, for British people who themselves were accustomed to seeing in the background only ships and voyages, the coast of France and pirates, and that what was quite ordinary for them would be distracting and confusing for us.

Serlo had to give way, and both agreed that as the play was in fact to be put on in a German theatre, this more serious and simpler background would best suit our type of imagination.

The casting had already been undertaken; Serlo took on Polonius, Aurelia Ophelia, Laertes had already been designated by his own name, and the part of Horatio was given to a thick-set, cheerful young man who had recently arrived; it was only in the case of the King and the Ghost that there was a certain embarrassment. For both parts there was only the Blustering Old Man. Serlo suggested that the Pedant should take the role of King; but Wilhelm protested most vigorously against this. They could not reach a decision.

What is more, Wilhelm had kept the two parts of Rosencrantz and Guildenstern in his play. 'Why haven't you joined these two together?' Serlo asked; 'after all, it's an abbreviation that can be effected so easily.'

'God preserve me from such curtailments which would do away with both the meaning and the effect!' Wilhelm replied. 'What these two men are and what they do can't be presented by *one* person. It is in such details that Shakespeare's greatness shows itself. This cautious way of proceeding, this perpetual climbing down, this yes-manship, this fondling and flattering, this adroitness, this fawning, this allness and emptiness, this legally proper villainy, this incapacity—how can it be expressed by means of *one* character? There should be at least a dozen of them, if they could be had; for they are something only in society, they are society, and Shakespeare was very modest and wise in only allowing two such representatives to appear in the play. Besides, I need them in my version as a couple, in contrast to the *one* good, first-rate Horatio.'

'I see what you mean,' said Serlo, 'and we can find a solution. We'll give the one part to Elmira' (this was the name of the eldest daughter of the Blustering Old Man); 'it can't do any harm for them to look well, and I will dress up the puppets and put them through their paces so that it will be a real treat.'

Philine was highly delighted at the prospect of having the role of the Player Queen in the play within the play. 'I will show people so naturally how someone takes a second husband in a hurry after she has been quite extraordinarily much in love with her first one,' she exclaimed. 'I hope to gain very great applause, and every man in the audience will want to be the third husband.'

Aurelia pulled a face at these remarks; her aversion for Philine increased daily.

'It really is a pity that we haven't any ballet,' Serlo said; 'otherwise you would be dancing a *pas de deux* for me with your first and second husbands, and the old man would fall asleep according to the measure, and your little feet and calves would look most charming over there at the back in the children's play.'

'Well, there's not much you know about my little calves,' she replied pertly, 'and as far as my feet are concerned, she cried out as she felt quickly under the table and fetched up her slippers, which she placed side by side in front of Serlo, 'here are the little stilts, and I give you the task of trying to find any that are prettier.'

'It was seriously meant,' he said, looking at the dainty shoes. Certainly it would not be easy to come across anything more finely designed.

They had been made in Paris; Philine had received them as a present from the Countess, a lady whose beautiful feet were famous.

'A charming object!' Serlo cried, 'My heart leaps up whenever I look at them.'

'What raptures!' Philine said.

'You can't beat a pair of slippers that have been made in so delicate and lovely manner,' Serlo rejoined, 'though their sound is still more charming than their appearance.' He lifted them up and dropped them a few times one after the other on to the table.

'What's that supposed to mean? Out with it!' Philine exclaimed.

'May I say,' he replied with mock modesty and waggish seriousness, 'that we bachelors, who for the most part are alone at night and yet have our fears like other people and long for company in the dark, especially in inns and strange places where things are somewhat uncanny, find it some consolation when a sweet child is willing to provide us with company and support. It is night-time, you are lying in bed, something rattles, you shudder, the door opens, you recognize a dear little whispering voice, something comes near, there is a swishing of curtains, click-clack, the shoes drop off, and in a flash you're no longer alone. Ah, that sweet, inimitable sound when the little heels knock on to the ground! The daintier they are, the more excellent it sounds. You can say what you like about Philomelas, about murmuring streams, about the whispering of the winds and about all the musical sounds you can think of, I go for click-clack! Click-clack is the loveliest theme for a rondo that you always want to hear all over again.'

Philine took the slippers out of his hands and said: 'Look how I have worn them out of shape! They are much too wide for me.' Then she played with them and rubbed the soles against one another. 'How hot it gets!' she exclaimed, as she held the one sole flat against her cheek; and then she rubbed it again and held it out to Serlo. He was good-natured enough to feel for the heat, when she cried out 'click-clack!' and gave him a sharp blow with the heel so that he drew back his hand with a shout. 'I'll teach you to get ideas into your head about my slippers,' Philine said with a laugh.

'And I'll teach you to treat old folk as if they were children!' Serlo replied, jumping up and taking hold of her impetuously, and stealing from her many a kiss, each of which she allowed to be snatched from her with artifice and with earnest reluctance. In the tussle her long hair came down and wound itself about the group, the chair was overturned and Aurelia, who felt inwardly offended by this mischief, stood up with displeasure.

Chapter Six

Although many characters had been dropped in the new adaption of *Hamlet*, the number that remained was still large enough, and the company was scarcely sufficient in size.

'If things go on like this,' said Serlo, 'our prompter will have to come up out of the prompter's box, mingle with us and become a character.'

'I've often admired him in his position,' Wilhelm rejoined.

'I don't believe that there is a more perfect prompter,' said Serlo. 'No one in the audience ever hears him; we on the stage understand every syllable. He has, so to speak, developed a special vocal organ for the purpose and is like a protective spirit that whispers audibly to us when we are in trouble. He senses which section of his part the actor knows perfectly, and from afar off has a presentiment when his memory is going to let him down. In some instances when I could scarcely read the part, he recited it to me word for word, and I could act it successfully; only he does have eccentricities which would make anybody else unusable: he reacts with so much feeling to the plays that he doesn't exactly declaim lofty passages, but he does recite them in an emphatic manner. This bad habit of his has led me astray more than once.'

'Just as he once left me high and dry at a very dangerous place because of another of his peculiarities,' Aurelia said.

'How was that possible, with his attentiveness?' Wilhelm asked.

'There are certain passages that affect him so much that he is moved to tears and completely loses his composure for some moments; and actually it is not the so-called pathetic passages that put him in this mood; it is, if I make myself clear, the *beautiful* passages, where the pure spirit of the poet, as it were, looks out from clear, open eyes, passages which bring at most pleasure to the rest of us and are received with indifference by many thousands.'

'And why doesn't he appear on the stage, as he has such a sensitive soul?'

'A hoarse voice and a stiff manner prevent him from being an actor, while his hypochondria excludes him from society,' Serlo went on. 'What trouble I have taken in order to get him used to myself—but in vain! He reads excellently, I've not heard anyone read like him; there is nobody who can keep to the delicate boundary-line between declamation and moving delivery as he does.'

'We've found him!' cried Wilhelm, 'we've found him! What a

fortunate discovery! Now we've got the actor who should recite for us the passage about the rugged Pyrrhus.'

'We need as much enthusiasm as you have, in order to make use of everything for its final purpose,' Serlo interposed.

'Indeed, I was most worried that this passage might have to be left out,' Wilhelm exclaimed, 'and that the whole play would suffer in consequence.'

'I can't see that, I must say,' Aurelia put in.

'I hope you will soon come round to my viewpoint,' Wilhelm said. 'Shakespeare introduces the arrival of the players with two aims in mind. In the first place the man who declaims the death of Pyrrhus with so much emotion of his own makes a deep impression on the Prince himself; he stirs the conscience of the vacillating young man: and in this way this scene acts as a prelude to the one in which the little play has such a great effect on the King. Hamlet feels put to shame by the actor who responds so sensitively to strange, fictitious suffering; and this at once arouses within him the thought of attempting to affect his stepfather's conscience. What a magnificent soliloquy it is that brings the second act to a close! How I am looking forward to reciting it:

> "O, what a rogue and peasant slave am I!
> Is it not monstrous that this player here,
> But in a fiction, in a dream of passion,
> Could force his soul so to his own conceit
> That from her working all his visage wann'd;
> Tears in his eyes, distraction in's aspect,
> A broken voice, and his whole function suiting
> With forms to his conceit? and all for nothing!
> For Hecuba!
> What's Hecuba to him, or he to Hecuba,
> That he should weep for her?" '

'If we can only get our man on to the stage,' Aurelia said.

'We shall have to bring him along to it gradually. At the rehearsals he can perhaps read the passage and we will say that we are expecting an actor who is to play the part, and so we shall see how we can get closer to him.'

After they had agreed about this, their conversation turned to the figure of the Ghost. Wilhelm could not make up his mind to leave to the Pedant the role of the living King so that the Blustering Old Man could play the Ghost, and he thought rather that they should wait for some time further, since after all some more actors had announced that they would be coming and the right man might well be found from them.

It can be imagined therefore how surprised Wilhelm was when he discovered on his table in the evening the following note, written with strange strokes of the pen, sealed up and addressed to him under his stage name:

'We know, oh singular young man, that you are in a great predicament. You can hardly find human beings for your *Hamlet*, let alone ghosts. Your zeal merits a miracle; we cannot work miracles, but something strange shall happen. If you have confidence, the Ghost will appear at the right hour. Have courage and stay calm! No answer is needed; your decision will be made known to us.'

He hurried back to Serlo with this strange piece of paper, and Serlo read it and re-read it, affirming in the end with a doubtful look that it was an important matter, and that they would no doubt have to consider whether they would be permitted to and be able to make such a venture; Aurelia was quiet, and smiled from time to time, and when the matter was talked about again a few days later, she intimated with some clarity that she took it to be a joke of Serlo's. She told Wilhelm not to worry at all and to wait patiently for the Ghost.

Altogether Serlo was in the best of humours; for the actors who were leaving soon made the greatest of efforts to perform well, so that they would be truly missed once they had gone, and he could expect that curiosity concerning the new company would lead to the best of box-office receipts.

Even associating with Wilhelm had had some influence on him. He began to talk more about art, for after all he was a German, and people of this nation like to give an account of what they do. Wilhelm made notes of many of these discussions; and as the narrative may not be interrupted so often here, we shall find another opportunity to present such essays on dramatic theory to those of our readers who are interested in them.

On one evening in particular Serlo was in a very gay mood when he was talking about the role of Polonius and how he was thinking of interpreting it. 'I promise that on this occasion I shall present a right worthy man; I shall demonstrate in a truly elegant way the appropriate qualities of composure and confidence, emptiness and importance, pleasantness and poor taste, liberty and oversight, sincere knavery and fabricated truth, and shall place them where they belong. I want to present and demonstrate, as politely as I can, this kind of drab, honest, persistent, time-serving semi-rogue, and for this purpose the somewhat rough and ready brush-strokes of our author will be of good service to me. I will talk like a book, when I've prepared myself, and like a fool, when I am in a good mood. I shall be insipid, so that I can fit in with everyone's views, and always refined enough not to notice when people are making a fool of me. It has not been easy for me to take over a role with such fun and roguishness.'

'If only I could hope for as much from mine,' Aurelia said. 'I am neither young nor gentle enough to be able to find my way into this character. One thing only I do know, unfortunately: the feeling that drives Ophelia crazy is one that won't leave me.'

'Let's not be so precise,' Wilhelm said; 'for, as a matter of fact, my wish to play Hamlet has led me very much astray, in spite of all my study of the play. The more I get into the part, the more I realize that in my whole appearance there is not a trace of the physiognomy that Shakespeare offers in his Hamlet. When I truly consider how exactly everything in the part hangs together, I scarcely trust myself to produce an effect that is tolerable.'

'You are embarking on your career with great conscientiousness,' put in Serlo. 'An actor fits into his part as best he can, and the part adjusts itself, as it must, to him. But what sort of a sketch has Shakespeare given of his Hamlet? Is he so very different from you?'

'In the first place Hamlet is blonde,' Wilhelm replied.

'I call that far-fetched,' said Aurelia. 'What makes you think that?'

'As a Dane, a man from the north, he is blonde from the start and has blue eyes.'

'Is Shakespeare supposed to have thought of that?'

'I can't find it specifically stated, but it seems to me to be undeniable when various references are taken together. He finds fencing hard-going, the sweat pours down off his face, and the Queen says: "He's fat and scant of breath." Can you think of him there except as blonde and portly? For dark-haired people are seldom like this when they are young. Do not his vacillating melancholy, his gentle sadness and his busy indecisiveness fit in better with that sort of a figure than when you imagine a slim youth with dark-brown hair, from whom we expect more decisiveness and agility?'

'You are upsetting my imagination', Aurelia exclaimed, 'Away with your fat Hamlet! We would rather be given any Tom, Dick or Harry who excites and moves us. The author's intention doesn't mean so much to us as our own pleasure, and what we require is a stimulus that is congenial to us.'

Chapter Seven

One evening the company was arguing as to whether the novel or the drama merited to be given preference. Serlo asserted that it was a futile controversy, based on misunderstanding; both could be excellent in their way, only they would have to keep within the limits of their genre.

'I'm not quite clear about it myself,' Wilhelm answered.

'Who is?' said Serlo, 'and yet it would be worth taking trouble to study the matter more closely.'

They talked a great deal this way and that, and in the end the results of their conversation were approximately as follows:

In the novel as in the drama we see human nature and human action. The difference in the two types of literature is not merely in external form, nor in the fact that in the one genre the characters talk while in the other genre they are usually talked about. Unfortunately, many plays are novels in dialogue form, and it would not be impossible to write a play consisting of letters.

In the novel it is primarily ways of thinking and events that are to be presented; in drama characters and deeds. The novel must move slowly, and the sentiments of the leading character must hold back, in whatever way this may be done, the forward-movement of the whole towards its fulfilment. Drama is to move rapidly, and the main character must press on towards the end, and only be delayed. The novel hero must be passive, or at least not in a high degree active; effect and action are expected from the dramatic hero. Grandison, Clarissa, Pamela, the Vicar of Wakefield, even Tom Jones himself are, if not passive in their effect, none the less characters of a retarding kind, and all the events are so to speak modelled according to their dispositions. In drama the hero does not model anything according to his own personality, everything resists him, and he either moves the obstacles out of his way or else is overcome by them.

They were also agreed that chance could be allowed to have its part in the novel, but that it must always be directed and guided by the dispositions of the characters; on the other hand that fate, which urges people on, without their assistance, through disconnected outward circumstances to an unforeseen catastrophe, only has a place in drama; that chance may be allowed to give rise to solemn, serious situations, but never to tragic ones; that fate on the other hand must always be terrible, and that it becomes tragic in the highest sense, when it brings together deeds that are guilty and innocent and independent of each other, into an unfortunate linkage.

These observations led once more to the strange *Hamlet* and to the peculiarities of this play. It was said that the hero in fact only has ways of thinking; what he encounters are only events that befall him, and in consequence the play has something of the extended quality of the novel; but because fate has sketched out the plan, because the play takes its start from a terrible deed and the hero is always being impelled forwards to a terrible deed, it is in the highest sense tragic and can tolerate no other but a tragic outcome.

Now a reading was to take place, and Wilhelm saw it in fact as a festive occasion. He had collated the parts in advance, so that there could be no difficulty from this point of view. All the players were familiar with the play, and he tried to convince them, before they started, of the importance of a reading. Just as we expect every musician to be able to play at sight to a certain extent, so every actor, indeed every well educated person, should practise sight-reading and should at once derive from a play, a poem or a short tale their essential quality and be able to present them with skill. No amount of memorizing will help if the actor has not in the first place penetrated into the spirit and mind of the good author; the letter can accomplish nothing.

Serlo assured the company that he would look to every other rehearsal, including the dress rehearsal, as soon as the reading had been given its due: 'for usually,' he said, 'nothing is more amusing than when actors talk about studying; it seems to me very much like freemasons talking about working.'

The reading took place as had been hoped, it can be said that the reputation and the good receipts of the company were based on these few well spent hours.

'You have done well, my friend,' Serlo said, when they were alone again, 'by talking to our colleagues in such a serious way, even though I fear that they will find it difficult to fulfil your wishes.'

'How do you mean?' Wilhelm rejoined.

'I have found,' said Serlo, 'that however easy it may be to stimulate peoples' imaginations and however gladly they like to be told fairy-tales, it is just as rarely that any kind of productive imagination can be found among them. In the case of actors this is very noticeable. Each of them is very happy to take on a fine, praiseworthy and brilliant part; but it is seldom that one of them does more than to put himself complacently in the hero's place without worrying in the least as to whether anyone would take him for the hero. But there are few who can grasp in lively fashion what the author had in mind in connection with the play, how much of their individuality they have to put in if they are to fill a part satisfactorily, how through their own conviction that they are some completely different person they may likewise be convincing to the audience, and how by means of the inner truth of the power of representation these boards may be transformed into temples and this cardboard into forests. Who can conceive of this inner strength of the spirit, which alone can deceive the audience, or of this fabricated truth, which alone is effective and induces illusion?

'Let us therefore not lay too much emphasis on spirit and emotion! The safest method is calmly to explain to our friends in the first place the literal meaning and to open their minds. He who has the natural talent will then himself develop quickly towards intelligent and sensitive expression; and he who lacks it will at least never act and recite in a completely misguided way. But I have found no worse presumption among actors, as among people in general, than when someone makes claims to know the spirit of a work while the letter is not yet clear and familiar to him.'

Chapter Eight

Wilhelm arrived very early for the first rehearsal in the theatre and discovered that he was on the stage on his own. The premises took him by surprise and brought back to him the strangest memories. The forest and village scenery was set up just as it had been on the stage of his home town, and also at a rehearsal when Mariane spiritedly avowed her love to him on that morning and agreed to spend the first happy night with him. The peasant cottages resembled one another on the stage as in the countryside; the true morning sun, coming through a half open window-shutter, shone upon part of a bench that was badly fixed by the door; only unfortunately it did not shine as on that former time on Mariane's bosom and lap. He sat down, thought about this amazing correspondence and believed that he could have a presentiment of seeing her again soon, perhaps at this place. Alas! And it was nothing more than the fact that an epilogue to which this scenery belonged was very frequently played in German theatres in those days.

He was disturbed in these considerations by the advent of the rest of the actors who were also accompanied by two friends of the stage and stage-wardrobe who greeted Wilhelm with enthusiasm.

The one was, as it were, attached to Madame Melina, but the other was a quite disinterested friend of the theatre arts, and both of them were the sort of friends that every good theatrical company should wish for. It was difficult to say whether they knew the theatre better than they loved it. They loved it too much to know it well; they knew it sufficiently to esteem what was good and to banish what was bad. But with their liking for the stage they did not find the mediocre unbearable, and the fine enjoyment with which they experienced, both in anticipation and after the event, what was good, was beyond all description. The mechanical features pleased them, the imaginative aspects delighted them, and their fondness was such that even a fragmented rehearsal induced in them a kind of sense of illusion. The shortcomings always seemed to withdraw into the distance, as far as they were concerned, while what was good touched them as if it were an object close at hand. In short they were dilettanti of the type that the specialist artist would very much like. Their favourite walk was from the wings to the stalls and from the stalls to the wings, their most pleasurable stay in the dressing-rooms, their most industrious occupation was to add some small touch to the stance, dress, recitation and delivery of the players, their liveliest conversation was about the effect that had been produced, and their most consistent efforts were devoted to keeping the actors attentive, active and precise, to doing things to please them or for their good, and to providing, though without lavishness, many a pleasure for the company. They had both procured for themselves the exclusive right to appear in the theatre during rehearsals and performances. As far as the production of *Hamlet* was concerned, they were not in agreement with Wilhelm at all points; he gave way here and there, but for the most part he maintained his position, and on the whole this type of discussion contributed a great deal to the cultivation of his taste. He let the two friends see how much he esteemed them, and they for their part prophesied nothing less from these concerted efforts than a new era in the German theatre.

The presence of these two men was very useful at rehearsals. In particular they convinced our actors of the need in rehearsals to combine position and movement continually with speech, in the way that it was proposed to demonstrate these during the performance, and of the need to link everything together mechanically through habit. During the rehearsal of a tragedy certainly, no commonplace gestures should be made, in particular with the hands; a tragic actor who took snuff in a rehearsal always made them anxious, they said, for he would most probably miss his pinch of snuff at a place like that during the performance. Indeed they contended that nobody should rehearse in boots if the part was to be played in shoes. But nothing grieved them more, they asserted, than when the ladies hid their hands in the folds of their dresses during rehearsals.

What is more, the exhortations of these men had one very good result, that is, that all the men learned to drill. 'As there are so many military roles,' they said, 'nothing looks more dismal than people who haven't the slightest military training swaggering about on the stage in the uniforms of captains and majors.'

Wilhelm and Laertes were the first to submit themselves to the tuition of a non-commissioned officer, and at the same time they continued their fencing exercises with great application.

The two men took so much trouble in training a company of actors that had come together so felicitously. They looked after the future satisfaction of the public, while the latter occasionally found fault with their marked dilettantism. People did not realize how much cause they had to be grateful to them, especially as they did not hesitate to impress frequently upon the actors the main point, that is, that it was their duty to speak loudly and audibly. In this they found more resistance and reluctance than they had at first thought. Most of them wanted to be heard as they spoke, and few took the trouble to speak in such a way that they could be heard. Some blamed the building for the failing, others said that you surely could not shout when you were expected to talk naturally, secretly or tenderly.

Our theatre friends, who were immensely patient, tried all ways of putting an end to this confusion and of dealing with this self-will. They did not hold back in giving reasons nor in making flattering remarks, and did finally achieve their aim, and the good example of Wilhelm was particularly helpful to them. He requested them to esconce themselves during rehearsals in the furthest corners and to knock against the seat with a key whenever they could not understand him completely. His articulation was good, he spoke in a moderate voice, gradually made the tone more emphatic, and did not strain his voice in the most fervent passages. With every rehearsal there was less to be heard from the knocking of keys; gradually the other members of the company came to tolerate the same procedure, and it was hoped that in the end the play would be audible to everybody in all corners of the house.

It can be seen from this example how gladly people would like to fulfil their purposes, but only in their own way, what trouble is needed in order to make comprehensible to them something that we take for granted, and how difficult it is to teach a person who wants to achieve something about the first conditions which alone make his project possible.

Chapter Nine

They now continued to go ahead with the necessary arrangements about scenery and costumes. Wilhelm had particular whims in connection with certain scenes and passages, and Serlo yielded here, partly because of the contract and partly from conviction, and because he hoped to win over Wilhelm with this complaisance and subsequently to direct all the more according to his own intentions.

Thus, for example, the King and Queen were to appear seated on their thrones at the first audience, with the courtiers standing at the sides and Hamlet unemphatically among them. 'Hamlet must comport himself quietly,' he said; 'his black clothing is already differentiation enough. He must, if anything, conceal himself rather than be prominent. It is only when the audience is finished and the King is talking with him as a son that he may step forward and that the scene may take its course.'

Another major difficulty was caused by the two pictures which Hamlet refers to so impetuously in the scene with his mother. 'As I see it, both should be life-size, and visible at the back of the room near the main door, and what is more, the old King must be hanging there in full armour like the Ghost, and on the same side that the Ghost enters. I want the figure in the picture to be assuming a commanding position with his right hand, to be turning somewhat and to be looking over his shoulder, so that he will completely resemble the Ghost at the moment when the latter goes out at the doorway. It will be very effective if at this moment Hamlet looks at the Ghost and the Queen looks at the picture. The stepfather can be displayed in royal array, but looking less significant than the old King.'

In this way various other points were brought up which we shall perhaps have an opportunity to talk about.

'Are you also adamant that Hamlet has to die in the end?' Serlo asked.

'How can I keep him alive,' said Wilhelm, 'when the whole play presses him on to death? After all we've already gone into this in detail.'

'But the public will want him alive.'

'I will gladly do any other favour for the audience, only this time it's impossible. We would be glad too if a good, useful man who is dying of a chronic illness could go on living longer. The family are in tears and implore the doctor, who can't do anything about it: and just as the doctor can't resist a physical necessity, so we likewise are unable to give our orders to an acknowledged artistic necessity. It is a false indulgence of the crowd to stimulate in them the emotions they want to feel and not those they ought to have.'

'He who pays the piper can call the tune.'

'To some extent; but a great public deserves to be respected and to be treated like children whose money people are after. By means of what is good the public should be gradually taught to have feeling and taste for what is good, and they will pay out their money with twice the pleasure because common sense and indeed discerning judgment itself will hold this expenditure against them. The public can be paid compliments like a beloved child, in order that it may be improved and at a future time enlightened; not like some elegant and rich person, in order to perpetuate the error that is being exploited.'

In this way they discussed a number of other things, in particular those concerning the question as to what further alterations might be made in the play and what would have to be left untouched. We are not going to go into further details about this now, but perhaps at some future date we may present the new adaptation of *Hamlet* itself to those of our readers who might possibly be interested in it.

Chapter Ten

The dress rehearsal was over; it had lasted an excessively long time. Serlo and Wilhelm found that there were still a number of things that had to be done, for in spite of the amount of time spent on preparations, some very necessary arrangements had been put off till the last minute.

Thus, for instance, the paintings of the two kings were not yet ready, and the scene between Hamlet and his mother, from which so much had been expected, still looked very thin, as neither the Ghost nor his painted likeness were to hand. Serlo joked about this, saying, 'We really should have been led up the garden-path if

the Ghost didn't turn up, if the watch really had to fight with thin
air, and if our prompter had to supply the Ghost's speech from the
wings.'

'We don't want to scare away our strange friend by our
scepticism,' Wilhelm answered; 'he is sure to come at the right
time and will take us by surprise as much as the audience.'

'Certainly I shall be glad when the play has been performed
tomorrow,' Serlo exclaimed; 'it's causing us more trouble than I
thought.'

'But nobody in the world will be happier than me when the play
has been put on tomorrow,' Philine replied, 'not that I am much
bothered by my part. The point is that I haven't patience to go on
listening all the time to one subject, and all that is to come out of
it is a perfomance which, like so many others, will be forgotten.
For God's sake don't make so much fuss! The guests who rise
from the dining-table have something critical to say afterwards
about every dish; indeed, when you hear them talking at home,
they can scarcely understand how they can have put up with such
hardship.'

'Let me make use of your image to my own advantage, sweet
child', Wilhelm answered. 'Think what nature and art must create
together, and business, machinery and trade, before a banquet
can be given. How many years must the deer spend in the forest,
and the fish in the river or sea, before they are worthy to occupy
our table, and what do not the housewife and the cook have to do
in the kitchen! How carelessly do we swallow over the dessert
what has been the care of the most distant vintner, of the sailor
and of the keeper of the wine-cellar, as if it had to be like this. And
should not, therefore, all these people work, be creative and make
their preparations, should not the master of the house bring and
keep everything carefully together, because in the last resort the
pleasure is only transient? But no pleasure is transient; for the
impression it leaves behind is lasting, and anything we do with
industry and effort communicates to the spectators a hidden
strength, the extent of whose influence we cannot judge.'

'It's all the same to me,' Philine replied, 'only I am made to
realize once again that men are always self-contradicting. For all
your conscientiousness in not wishing to mutilate the great
author, you none the less leave the finest thought out of the play.'

'The finest?' Wilhelm exclaimed.

'Indeed the finest, one that Hamlet himself is rather proud of.'

'And what might that be?' Serlo exclaimed.

'If you had a wig on,' Philine replied, 'I would quite neatly and
cleanly take it off you; for it seems necessary that somebody
should open up your intelligence for you.'

The others reflected, and the conversation came to a halt. They had got up from their seats, it was already late, they seemed to want to disperse. As they stood there so undecidedly, Philine started to sing a little song which had a very dainty and pleasing tune.

> Sing no more with sounds of sadness
> Of the loneliness of night;
> No, it's made, O lovely ladies,
> For sociability's delight.
>
> If to be his better portion
> Woman was designed for man.
> So the night is half our lifetime,
> and the finest part in the plan.
>
> Can the day-time give you pleasure?
> It only breaks up your delight.
> It will do to pass the time in,
> For all else, though, it's not right.
>
> But when through the hours of night-time
> The sweet lamp's pretty twilight glows,
> And from mouth to mouth so closely
> Loving entertainment flows;
>
> When the quick and wanton fellow,
> Otherwise enflamed and wild,
> Often lingers for a token
> With amusements that are mild;
>
> When the nightingale greets lovers
> With a song where love abounds,
> To the captives and the wretched
> The song has only sorrowful sounds.
>
> With what gentle inward striving
> You may hear the bell that rings,
> Offering with twelve measured pulses
> Peaceful and trustworthy things.
>
> Therefore as the long day passes,
> O my heart, keep this in sight:
> Every day has its vexation,
> And the night-time its delight.

She gave a little bow when she had finished, and Serlo called to her with a loud 'Bravo.' She bounded out of the room and hastened away laughing. She could be heard singing as she went down the stairs, and there was the clattering of her heels.

Serlo went into the adjoining room, and Aurelia remained standing for a few moments longer with Wilhelm, who was saying good-night to her, and she said:

'How I dislike her! She is really antipathetic to my inner being, right down to the smallest chance details. The dark eyelashes of her right eye along with blonde hair are something I don't like to look at, though my brother finds them so attractive, and the scar on her forehead has for me something so repugnant and common about it that I always feel like taking ten steps back from her. She was telling a story recently as a joke about the way her father threw a plate at her head when she was a child, and that she still bears the mark of it. Certainly there are marks near her eyes and on her forehead to the right, and they are of such a sort that you feel like being on guard against them.'

Wilhelm did not answer, and Aurelia seemed to continue with more resentment:

'It is almost impossible for me to exchange a friendly and polite word with her, I hate her so much, and yet she is so ingratiating. I wish we were rid of her. You too, my friend, treat this creature with a certain favour, this is behaviour which wounds me to the quick, an attention bordering on respect, and something, by God, that she doesn't deserve!'

'The way she is, I owe her thanks all the same', Wilhelm replied; 'her behaviour is blameworthy; but I must let justice be done to her character.'

'Character!' Aurelia exclaimed; 'Do you think that a creature like that has a character? O you men, that's how I recognize you! You deserve women like that!'

'Are you suspicious of me, my friend?' Wilhelm replied. 'I am willing to account for every minute which I have spent with her.'

'Very well now,' Aurelia said, 'it's late, we don't want to quarrel. One and all, they are all the same! Good night, my friend! Good night, my fine bird of paradise!'

Wilhelm asked why he was given this title of honour.

'Some other time,' Aurelia replied, 'some other time. It was said that they had no feet, hovered about in the air and lived on air. But it's a fairy-tale,' she continued, 'a poetic fiction. Good night, see that you have sweet dreams, if you're lucky.'

She went into her room and left him on his own; he hurried to his room.

He walked up and down, feeling somewhat indignant. Aurelia's jocular, but decisive tone had offended him; he felt deeply what an

injustice she was doing him. He could not treat Philine unkindly,
as if she were repugnant to him; she had done nothing wrong as
far as he was concerned, and then for his part he felt so far
removed from any special liking for her that he could face his own
self-criticism with real pride and firmness.

He was just going to undress, go to his bed and open the
curtains when to his very great astonishment he saw a pair of
ladies' slippers in front of the bed; the one was standing, the other
one was lying. They were Philine's slippers, which he recognized
only too well; he thought also that he could detect some disarray
about the curtains, indeed it seemed as if they were moving; he
stood and looked in that direction with unblinking eyes.

A new feeling, which he took to be annoyance, made him catch
his breath; and after a short pause in which he had recovered
himself he called out in a composed manner:

'Get up, Philine! What does this mean? What has happened to
your good sense, your good behaviour? Are we to be the talk of the
house in the morning?'

There was no movement.

'I'm not joking,' he went on, 'I don't like this sort of teasing.'

Not a sound, not a movement!

Finally he went up to the bed, in determined and ill-humoured
mood, and pulled the curtains apart. 'Get up,' he said, 'unless I
am to vacate the room to you for the night.'

To his great surprise he found that his bed was empty and that
the pillows and bed-coverings were in perfect and calm order. He
looked round, searched about, went through everything and
found not a trace of the wag. There was nothing to be seen behind
the bed, the stove or the wardrobes; he looked more and more
diligently; indeed, a malicious onlooker might have been inclined
to believe that he was searching in order to find.

He could not sleep; he put the slippers on to his table, walked
up and down, came to a halt at the table a number of times, and a
roguish spirit that was watching him is willing to assert that he
spent a large part of the night occupied with the most delightful of
little stilts, that he looked at them, handled them and played with
them with a certain interest, and that it was not until nearly
morning that he threw himself fully dressed on to the bed, where
he went to sleep amid the strangest imaginings.

And in fact he was still sleeping when Serlo came in and said:
'Where are you? Still in bed? Impossible! I've been looking for you
in the theatre, where there are still quite a lot of things to do.'

Chapter Eleven

Morning and afternoon went quickly by. The auditorium was already full, and Wilhelm hastened to get changed. He could not now assume the disguise with the easy feeling that he had had when he first tried the costume on; he got dressed in order to be ready. When he joined the ladies in the assembly room they told him with one accord that nothing was put on properly; the fine tuft of feathers was out of place, and the buckle was unsuitable; they again started to pull apart, to sew and to put together. The overture began, Philine had some criticism to make of the ruffle, Aurelia found much wrong with the cloak. 'Let me be, children!' he exclaimed, 'it is this negligent touch that really makes me into Hamlet.' The women did not let him go and continued to smarten him up. The overture had finished, and the play had begun. He looked at himself in the mirror, pressed the hat down lower over his face, and renewed the make-up.

At that moment someone rushed in crying 'The Ghost! The Ghost!'

The whole day through Wilhelm had not had time to think of the main worry, that is, whether the Ghost really would come. Now the anxiety had completely gone, and the strangest guest-performance was to be expected. The manager came and asked about this and that; Wilhelm did not have time to look around for the Ghost, and he only hurried in order to find his place by the throne, where the King and Queen were already surrounded by their court and were resplendent in all their magnificence; he only caught the last words of Horatio who spoke about the appearance of the Ghost in quite a confused manner and seemed as if he had almost forgotten his part.

The drop-curtain went up, and he saw the full house before him. After Horatio had made his speech and had been dismissed by the King, he pressed close to Hamlet and as if he were presenting himself to him, the Prince, he said: 'it's the devil who's inside that armour! He's put fear into all of us.'

In the meantime all that could be seen was two tall men in white cloaks and hoods who were standing in the wings, and Wilhelm, whose first soliloquy had been a failure, as he thought, in the distraction, unrest and confusion, came on to the stage for the terrible, dramatic winter's night in a truly uneasy mood, although vigorous applause had accompanied him when he had gone off. However, he pulled himself together and spoke the passage, purposely with the appropriate indifference, forgot the

Ghost, as did the audience, in the process, and really did take fright when Horatio exclaimed 'Look, my Lord, it comes!' He turned round with a sudden movement, and the tall, noble figure, the gentle, inaudible step, and light movement in the heavy-looking armour made so strong an impression upon him that he stood there as if petrified and could exclaim 'Angels and ministers of grace defend us!' only with half a voice. He stared at the figure, drew breath several times and delivered the address to the Ghost in so confused, fragmented and forced a manner that the greatest art could not have expressed the speech so excellently.

His translation of this passage helped him greatly. He had kept close to the original, whose word order seemed to him to present in a unique way the state of mind of someone who has been taken by surprise, terrified and seized by terror.

> Be thou a spirit of health|or goblin damn'd,
> Bring with thee airs from heaven or blasts from hell,
> Be thy intents wicked or charitable,
> Thou comest in such a questionable shape
> That I will speak to thee: I'll call thee Hamlet,
> King, father, royal Dane: O answer me!

It could be sensed that there was a very great effect taking place in the audience. The Ghost beckoned, the Prince followed him amidst the loudest applause.

The scene changed, and when they came to the distant place the Ghost stopped unexpectedly and turned round; as a result Hamlet came to be standing rather too close to him. Wilhelm at once looked with desire and curiosity between the lowered visor, but could only see deep-set eyes and a well shaped nose. He stood before him peering fearfully; but when the first sounds came forth from the helmet, when a harmonious, only slightly rough voice could be heard saying 'I am thy father's spirit,' Wilhelm stepped back a few paces shuddering, and the whole audience shuddered. The voice seemed known to everybody, and Wilhelm believed he could notice a similarity with his father's voice. Wilhelm was pulled in contrary directions by these strange feelings and memories, by the curiosity to discover who the strange friend was, by fear of offending him, and even by the impropriety of approaching him as an actor too closely in this situation. During the Ghost's long narrative he changed his position so often, and seemed so vague and embarrassed, so attentive and so distracted, that his acting aroused general admiration, just as the Ghost stirred up general terror. The latter spoke more with a deep feeling of annoyance rather than of misery, but it was a slow, unbounded, spiritual annoyance. It was the despondence of a great soul which is separated from all that is earthly and yet collapses beneath infinite sufferings. In the end the Ghost sank down, but in a strange manner: for a light, transparent, grey gauze which seemed to rise like steam from the aperture spread over him and drew him down with it.

Now Hamlet's friends came back and swore on the sword. Here the old mole worked so busily in the earth that he kept on calling out 'Swear' to them from beneath their feet, wherever they might be standing, and they hurried quickly from one place to another, as if the ground were burning beneath them. Furthermore, on each occasion a little flame appeared out of the ground where they were standing, intensified the effect and made the deepest impression on all spectators.

Now the play took its course irresistibly, nothing went wrong, everything succeeded; the audience demonstrated its satisfaction; with every scene the enjoyment and the confidence of the actors seemed to increase.

Chapter Twelve

The curtain fell, and the most lively applause resounded from all parts. The four princely corpses leapt nimbly up and embraced one another with joy. Polonius and Ophelia also came out of their graves and were able to hear with lively pleasure how Horatio, when he came forward to announce the forthcoming theatre programme, was applauded most vigorously. The audience did not want to let him announce any other play, but stormily demanded the repetition of that night's play.

'Now we've won,' Serlo exclaimed, 'but no more serious words this evening! Everything depends on the first impression. No actor should be reproached if he is cautious and self-willed at his first appearance.'

The cashier came and handed a heavy cash-box over to him. 'We've had a good first night,' he called out, 'and prejudice will be in our favour. Now where is the promised evening meal? Today we can let ourselves really enjoy it.'

They had agreed that they would remain together in their stage costumes and would have a celebration among themselves. Wilhelm had undertaken to prepare the setting and Madame Melina the food.

A room, which was normally used for painting in, had been very specially cleaned up and re-arranged with all kinds of little decorations and so set off that it looked half like a garden, half like a colonnade. As they came in, the company was dazzled by the brilliance of many lights which diffused a solemn glow over a well decked and well set table through the fumes of the sweetest incense, and people took their seats with dignity; it seemed as if a royal family were coming together in the realm of the spirits. Wilhelm sat between Aurelia and Madame Melina, Serlo between Philine and Elmira; nobody was dissatisfied with himself nor with his place at the table.

The two theatre friends who had likewise appeared added to the happiness of the company. In the course of the performance they had come on to the stage several times, and they could not speak highly enough of their own satisfaction and that of the audience; then they went on to particularize; each person was richly rewarded for his contribution.

With incredible vivacity one merit after another and one place after another were thrown into relief. The prompter, who sat modestly at the end of the table, was highly praised for his rugged Pyrrhus; the fencing of Hamlet and Laertes could not be sufficiently extolled; Ophelia's sadness was beautiful and noble beyond all words; nothing at all was allowed to be said about Polonius's acting; everyone present heard his own praise in and through the other.

But the absent Ghost also received his share of praise and admiration. He had spoken the part in a very felicitous voice and with a great sense of meaning, what surprised them most was that he seemed to be informed of everything that had taken place within the company. He fully resembled the painted picture, as if he had posed for the artist, and the theatre friends could not praise sufficiently his terrifying appearance when he had stepped forward not far from the painting and had strode past his likeness. Truth and error mingled so strangely there, they said, and people had really been convinced that the Queen could not see the one figure. Madame Melina was much praised in the context, since she had stared upward at the picture at this juncture, while Hamlet had been pointing downwards to the Ghost.

They inquired how the Ghost could have crept in, and learnt from the theatre manager that two tall figures in white cloaks and hoods who could not be distinguished from one another had come in at the rear door which was usually obstructed with scenery, but which had been unblocked this evening because the company had needed the gothic hall; and they had presumably gone out again at the end of the third act by this way too.

Serlo praised the Ghost especially because he had not wailed so timorously and right at the end in fact he had brought in a passage which was more suited to such a great hero for stirring his son to action. Wilhelm had retained it in his memory and promised to transcribe it into the manuscript.

In the gaiety of the banquet they had not noticed that the children and the Harpist were missing; but the latter soon made an appearance in a very pleasant manner. For they came in together, dressed up very fantastically, Felix was striking a triangle, Mignon a tambourine, and the old man had slung the heavy harp about him and was playing it while carrying it before him. They walked in procession round the table and sang all kinds of songs. They were given food, and the guests believed that they were showing the children a kindness if they gave them as much sweet wine as they wanted to drink; for the company themselves had not been sparing of the delicious bottles which had arrived this evening in some baskets as a present from the theatre friends. The children kept on jumping about and singing, and Mignon in particular was exuberant; she had never been seen like this before. She beat the tambourine with all possible grace and liveliness; now she moved her finger quickly this way and that on the skin, exerting pressure, now she knocked on it with the back of her hand or with her knuckles, indeed with varying rhythms she banged the parchment now against her knees and now against her head, while at another time she made shaking movements that caused the little bells to sound on their own, and in this way she enticed quite varied sounds out of the very simple instrument. After they had been noisy for quite a time they sat down in an arm-chair which had remained empty just facing Wilhelm at the table.

'Stay away from the chair!' Serlo called out, 'it's put there for the Ghost presumably; if he comes, things may go badly with you.'

'I'm not afraid of him,' Mignon cried, 'if he comes, we will get up. It's my uncle, he won't harm me.' Nobody could understand this comment except someone who knew that she had called her supposed father the 'big devil.'

People in the company looked at one another and felt even more strengthened in their suspicion that Serlo knew something about the Ghost's manifestation. They chatted and drank, and the girls looked timidly from time to time towards the door.

Sitting in the big chair and peeping out over the table, but only like Pulcinello dolls out of the box, the children began to perform in this way a play. Mignon imitated the humming sound very prettily, and finally they knocked their heads together to such an extent, banging them also on the edge of the table, in a way that only wooden puppets can tolerate. Mignon was merry to the point of anger, and the company had to call her to a halt in the end, however much they had laughed at the joke at first. But talking did not help much, for she now jumped up and raced round the table with the tambourine in her hand. Her hair was flying and as she threw back her head and so to speak tossed all her limbs into the air, she seemed like a Maenad whose wild and almost impossible positions still surprise us frequently on old monuments.

Aroused by the talents of the children and by their noise, everyone sought to contribute something to the entertainment of the company. The ladies sang some canons, Laertes caused a nightingale's song to be heard, and the Pedant performed a pianissimo concerto on the Jew's harp. Meanwhile those who were neighbours at table played all sorts of games where hands meet and intertwine, and in the case of several couples there was no lack of expressions of hopeful fondness. Madame Melina in particular appeared not to be concealing a lively inclination towards Wilhelm. It was late at night, and Aurelia, who almost alone had still retained control over herself, admonished the others to go home, and rose herself.

As they were going, Serlo gave an imitation of a firework display, able as he was, in an almost incomprehensible way, to render the sound of rockets, squibs and Catherine-wheels. One only had to close one's eyes for the illusion to be complete. Meanwhile everyone had got up, and the gentlemen offered their arms to the ladies in order to escort them home. Wilhelm went last with Aurelia. On the stairway they met the theatre manager who said, 'Here is the veil in which the Ghost disappeared. It had got caught in the trap-door, and we have just found it.' 'A strange relic,' Wilhelm exclaimed and took it from him.

At that moment he felt himself being seized by the left arm and at the same time he experienced a very intense pain. Mignon had been hiding, had grasped hold of him and bitten into his arm. She went past him down the stairs and disappeared.

When the company came into the fresh air, almost everyone noticed that they had been having too much of a good thing that evening. Without taking leave, they went their various ways.

Wilhelm had scarcely reached his room when he threw off his clothes and hurried to bed after extiguishing the light. Sleep was about to overpower him straight away; but a noise that seemed to originate in his room behind the stove made him pay attention. The image of the King in armour was just then poised before his heated imagination; he sat up in order to address the ghostly figure, when he was aware of being embraced by soft arms, as his mouth was closed with lively kisses, and he felt a breast pressing against his own which he had not the courage to repulse.

Chapter Thirteen

Next morning Wilhelm started up with an uncomfortable feeling and found his bed empty. His head was heavy as he had not fully slept off the effects of drinking, and the memory of the unknown nocturnal visitor disturbed him. His first suspicion fell on Philine, and yet it did not seem as if the lovely body that he had held in his arms had been hers. Amid lively caresses our friend had gone to sleep by the side of this strange silent visitor, and now no further trace of her was to be found. He leapt up, and while he was getting dressed he found that his door, which he usually bolted, was only ajar, and he could not remember whether he had locked it the previous evening.

But what seemed most strange to him was the Ghost's veil which he found on his bed. He had brought it up with him and had presumably thrown it there himself. It was a grey gauze, and at its edge he saw some writing with black letters stitched on. He unfolded it and read the words: 'For the first and last time, take flight! Young man, take flight!' He was taken aback and did not know what he should say.

At that very moment Mignon came in bringing breakfast. Wilhelm was surprised at the child's appearance, indeed it may be said he was startled. She seemed to have become bigger during the night; she stepped in front of him with a lofty, noble propriety and looked into his eyes with great seriousness, so that he could not bear her gaze. She did not touch him as at other times when she usually pressed his hand and kissed him on the cheek, mouth, arm or shoulder, but went silently away again after tidying his things.

The time now came for a play-reading that had been fixed; they came together, and were all out of sorts because of the previous day's festivities. Wilhelm pulled himself together as well as he could, in order that he should not right at the beginning go against the principles that he had been preaching so vigorously. His good training helped him through; for in all the arts training and habit must stop up the gaps which would so often be left by genius and whim.

Actually, however, on this occasion it would be possible to find much truth in the observation that no position that might last a fair length of time, and in fact become a profession and a way of life, should be allowed to start off with some form of solemn occasion; all ceremonies held at the start of a project exhaust the enjoyment and energetic force which should elicit the sense of endeavour and support us in circumstances of continued effort. Of all festivities wedding celebrations are the most inappropriate; none should be performed more than these in quietness, humility and hope.

Thus the day now crept on, and no day had ever seemed to Wilhelm up to now to be so ordinary. Instead of the usual conversation in the evening people started yawning; interest in *Hamlet* had been exhausted, and it was discovered to be irksome rather than anything else that it was to be performed a second time on the next day. Wilhelm showed people the Ghost's veil; from this it had to be concluded that the Ghost would not come again. Serlo in particular supported this opinion; he seemed to be very familiar with the advice of the strange figure; on the other hand the words 'Take flight! Young man, take flight!' could not be explained. How could Serlo be in agreement with someone who seemed to have the aim of removing the most outstanding actor in his company?

So it was necessary to give the part of the Ghost to the Blustering Old Man and that of the King to the Pedant. Both declared that they were already acquainted with the parts, and this was no wonder, since everybody had become so familiar with the play in the course of the many rehearsals and the extended discussions that they could all have changed roles quite easily. However, they quickly went through some parts of the play, and when they separated, at a late enough hour, Philine whispered softly to Wilhelm on parting: 'I must fetch my slippers; you are not going to bolt the door, are you?' When he came to his room these words put him into a position of some embarrassment; for the assumption that his previous night's guest had been Philine was strengthened by them, and we too are compelled to join in with this opinion, especially as we cannot discover the reasons which made him doubtful about it and could not but induce in him another particular suspicion. He walked restlessly up and down in his room a few times and really had not as yet bolted the door.

All at once Mignon rushed into the room, seized hold of him and shouted, 'Master! Save the house! It's on fire!' Wilhelm leapt to the door, and a powerful gust of smoke pressed down towards him from the upper stairway. In the street shouts of 'fire!' could already be heard, and the Harpist came breathlessly through the smoke down the stairs, with his instrument in his hand. Aurelia rushed out of her room and threw little Felix into Wilhelm's arms. 'Save the child!' she cried; 'we will look after the other things.'

Wilhelm, who did not believe the danger was so great, thought at first that he would press through to the origin of the fire, so that he might perhaps be able to extinguish it while it was still in its initial stages. He gave the child to the old man and ordered him to hurry down the winding staircase of stone which led into the garden through a little cellar, and so to stay out of doors with the children. Mignon took a light in order to show him the way. Then Wilhelm asked Aurelia to rescue her own things by the same route. He himself penetrated upwards through the smoke; but it was in vain that he exposed himself to danger. The flames seemed to be coming over from the neighbouring house and had already set fire to the woodwork of the floor and to a small stairway; others who hurried along to assist in rescue work suffered, as he did, from the thick smoke and the fire. However, he spoke encouraging words to them and called for water; he implored them only to retreat from the flames step by step, and promised to stay with them. At that moment Mignon came up, shouting, 'Master! Save your Felix! The old man has gone mad! The old man is killing him!' Without further thought Wilhelm leapt down the stairs, and Mignon followed at his heels.

He halted aghast on the last steps leading into the cellar. Large bundles of straw and brushwood, which had been collected in piles there, were burning with bright flames; Felix was lying on the ground screaming; the old man was standing sideways by the wall, with head bowed. 'What are you doing, unhappy man?' cried Wilhelm. The old man was silent, Mignon had picked Felix up and was dragging the boy with difficulty into the garden, while Wilhelm was making efforts to pull the burning material apart and to extinguish the fire, but in so doing only increased the force and vigour of the flames. In the end he too had to take flight into the garden, with scorched eyebrows and hair, at the same time pulling with him through the flames the old man who reluctantly followed him and whose beard was singed.

Wilhelm hurried immediately to look for the children in the garden. He found them on the threshold of a distant summer-house, and Mignon was doing her best to pacify the little one. Wilhelm took him on his lap, questioned him, felt him, and could not get anything coherent out of either of the children.

In the meantime the fire in its fury had seized several houses and was lighting up the whole area. Wilhelm inspected the child by the red light of the flames; he could not observe any wounds or blood, nor yet any bruises. He felt the child all over, he did not give any sign of being in pain, indeed he gradually calmed down and began to marvel at the flames, in fact to take pleasure at the beautiful rafters and beams as they burnt one after the other like a festive illumination.

Wilhelm did not think of the clothes and other things that he could have lost; he felt strongly how precious these two human creatures were to him, now that he had seen that they had escaped from so great a danger. He pressed the little boy to his heart with a quite new emotion, and wanted to embrace Mignon also with happy fondness, but she gently refused this, took him by the hand and held it fast.

'Master,' she said (never before this evening had she given him this name, for at first she was accustomed to calling him 'sir' and later 'father'), 'Master! We have escaped from a great danger: your Felix was close to death.'

After many questions Wilhelm at last found out that when they had entered the cellar the Harpist had snatched the light from her hand and at once set fire to the straw. Then he had put Felix down, placed his hands on the child's head amid strange gestures and taken a knife, as if he wanted to sacrifice him. Mignon reported how she had intervened and had pulled the knife out of his hand; she had shouted, and somebody from the house, who had been saving some things and bringing them out to the garden, had come to her help; but in the confusion he must have gone away again and left the old man and the child on their own.

Two or three houses were fully ablaze. Nobody had been able to escape out into the garden on account of the fire in the cellar. Wilhelm was more embarrassed because of his friends than on account of his things. He did not dare to leave the children and saw the disaster continually increasing.

He spent some hours in an anxious situation. Felix had fallen asleep on his lap, Mignon was lying by his side, holding his hand tightly. Eventually the measures taken had put a stop to the fire. The gutted buildings collapsed, morning came, the children were beginning to freeze, and in his light clothing he himself found the falling dew almost unbearable. He took them to the ruins of the building that had fallen down, and they found a very comforting warmth by a heap of cinders and ashes.

The dawning new day gradually brought all friends and acquaintances together now. Everyone had escaped, nobody had lost much.

Wilhelm's trunk was also found again, and, when it was getting on for ten o'clock, Serlo insisted on having a rehearsal of *Hamlet*, at least of a few scenes which had been manned with new actors. After that he still had a number of debates with the police. The clergy were demanding that after such a divine judgment the theatre should stay closed, and Serlo maintained that the performance of an interesting play was more appropriate than ever, partly for the replacement of what he had lost in the night, and partly in order to cheer up people's terrified spirits. This latter view was the one that prevailed, and the house was full. The actors performed with rare and greater passion than the first time. The audience was more receptive to extraordinary features, their feelings having been intensified by the terrible night-scene and excited even more at the prospect of an interesting entertainment because of the boredom of a day that had been spoilt and full of distractions. Most of the audience consisted of new spectators who had been attracted by the reputation of the play and who could make no comparisons with the first evening's performance. The Blustering Old Man acted his part completely in the spirit of the unknown Ghost, and the Pedant likewise had paid good attention to his predecessor; what is more, his wretchedness was very useful to him, so that Hamlet was really not doing him an injustice when he called him a king of shreds and patches in spite of his purple robe and ermine collar.

Perhaps no one had attained the throne more strangely than he; and although the others, especially Philine, made much fun of his new dignity, he none the less indicated that the Count, as a great connoisseur, had predicted as much and even more of him at first sight; Philine on the other hand admonished him to humility and asserted that he should be reminded of that unhappy night at the castle and should wear the crown with modesty.

Chapter Fourteen

The members of the company had looked round in haste for lodgings and had been very much preoccupied in consequence. Wilhelm had grown fond of the summer-house in the garden where he had spent the night; he had no difficulty in obtaining the key to it and settled in there; but as Aurelia was very short of space in her new accommodation, he had to keep Felix by his side, and Mignon did not want to be parted from the boy.

The children had been installed in a pleasant room on the first floor, while Wilhelm had occupied the lower room. The children slept, but he could not find rest.

Adjoining the agreeable garden, which was magnificently lit up by the newly risen full moon, stood the sad ruins from which smoke was still rising here and there; the air was pleasant and the night unusually beautiful. While leaving the theatre, Philine had touched his elbow and whispered a few words to him, but he had not understood them. He was confused and annoyed, and did not know what he should expect or do. Philine had been avoiding him for some days and had only given him a sign again on this particular evening. The door which he was not to bolt was now unfortunately burnt down, and the little slippers had gone up in smoke. How the lovely woman was to come into the garden, if this was her intention, he did not know. He did not wish to see her, and yet he would have been only too willing to explain himself to her.

But what weighed upon him more heavily was the fate of the Harpist who had not been seen again. Wilhelm was afraid that he might be found dead under the débris when it came to clearing up the rubble. Wilhelm had concealed from everyone the suspicion which he harboured, that the old man was responsible for the fire. For he had first met him as he came from the burning and smoking ground level, and the mood of despair in the cellar seemed to be the consequence of such an unfortunate event. Yet in the course of the investigation, which the police at once undertook, it had become likely that the fire had originated not in the house where they had been living, but in the third of these houses, and that also it had at once slipped along under the roofs.

Wilhelm was considering all this as he sat in a bower, when he heard someone moving quietly in a nearby passage. He recognized that it was the Harpist by the song that he at once began to sing. The song, which he could understand very clearly, portrayed the consolation of an unhappy person who feels that he is quite close to madness. Unfortunately Wilhelm only remembered its last verse.

> I will creep along past doorways,
> Pause with quiet and modesty,
> Food from pious hands will reach me,
> And I'll go on readily.
> Each will think himself so happy,
> When my figure comes in view,
> You will see him let a tear fall,
> I can't tell to what it's due.

While these words were being sung, he had come to the garden door which led to a quiet street; as he found it closed, he tried to climb over by the trellis-work; but Wilhelm held him back and talked to him in a friendly way. The old man begged him to open the door because he wished to and had to take flight. Wilhelm explained to him that he might well be able to escape from the garden, but not from the town, and showed him how suspicious he would make himself look if he took such a step; but in vain! The old man insisted on his intention. Wilhelm did not yield and in the end pushed him partly by force into the summer-house, shut himself in with him there and conducted a strange conversation with him, which we, however, prefer to pass over silently rather than to communicate in detail, in order not to torment our readers with disconnected and anxious emotions.

Chapter Fifteen

On that very same morning Laertes rescued Wilhelm from the great embarrassment he was in as to what he should do with the unfortunate old man who was showing such evident signs of madness. Laertes who, according to his old custom, was in the habit of going about everywhere had seen a man in the coffee-house who had been suffering the most acute attacks of melancholy some time previously. He had been entrusted to a country clergyman who made it a special calling of his to care for people of this sort. He had been successful on this occasion too; he was still in the town, and the family of the man who had been cured held him in great respect.

Wilhelm at once hurried to visit the man, told him about the case and came to an arrangement with him. By means of certain pretexts it was possible to hand over the old man to him. The parting caused Wilhelm great grief, and only the hope of seeing him restored to health could make the separation to some extent bearable for him, for he was so accustomed to seeing the man about him and to hearing the gifted and heartfelt sounds of his music. The harp had burnt in the fire; another one was procured, which he was given to take with him on the journey.

The fire had also consumed Mignon's little wardrobe, and when it came to preparing to obtain new things for her again, Aurelia made the suggestion that surely it was time now to dress her as a girl.

'No, not now at all!' Mignon exclaimed, and she insisted on her old style of dress with great vigour, and in this they had to let her have her way.

The company did not have much time to be reflective; the performances took their course.

Wilhelm often listened for the public's reactions, and it was only rarely that he came across an opinion of the type that he wanted to hear, indeed he often heard what saddened or annoyed him. Thus for instance, immediately after the first performance of *Hamlet*, a young man reported with great vivacity how satisfied he had been that evening in the theatre. Wilhelm listened and heard to his great confusion that the young man, to the irritation of the people sitting behind him, had kept his hat on and had obstinately refused to take it off throughout the entire performance, which heroic action he recalled with the greatest pleasure.

Someone else maintained that Wilhelm had played the part of Laertes very well; on the other hand, it was difficult to be as contented with the actor who had taken on Hamlet. This mistake was not entirely unnatural, for Wilhelm and Laertes did resemble each other, even if in a very remote way.

A third person praised his acting most highly, especially in the scene with his mother, and only regretted that just at that ardent moment a white ribbon had been showing under his waistcoat, and that in consequence the illusion had been very much destroyed.

Within the company itself meanwhile all sorts of changes were taking place. Since that evening after the fire Philine had not given Wilhelm even the slightest indication of an approach on her part. She had rented more distant lodgings, it seemed as if intentionally, was living harmoniously with Elmira and came less frequently to Serlo, which undoubtedly pleased Aurelia. Serlo, who continued to be favourably inclined to her, sometimes visited her, especially as he hoped to find Elmira with her, and one evening he took Wilhelm with him. Both were very surprised, as they went in, to see Philine in the further room in the arms of a young officer who was wearing a red uniform and white underclothes; however, they could not see his face that was turned away from them. Philine came towards her visiting friends in the ante-room and closed the other one. 'You surprise me in the course of a strange adventure!' she exclaimed.

'It isn't all that strange,' Serlo said; 'let us see your handsome, enviable young friend; in any case, you have already put us so much in our places that we are not permitted to be jealous.'

'I must leave you with this suspicion for some time longer', Philine said jokingly; 'but I can assure you that it is only a young lady, a good friend who wishes to stay with me incognito for a few days. You shall learn about her fortunes at some future time, indeed perhaps you will yourselves become acquainted with the interesting girl, and then I shall presumably have reason to exercise my modesty and complaisance; for I am afraid that the gentlemen will forget their old friend on account of their new acquaintance.'

Wilhelm stood petrified; for rightaway at the first glimpse, the red uniform had reminded him of Mariane's coat that he had loved so much; it was her figure and her blonde hair, only the present officer seemed to him to be somewhat taller.

'For heaven's sake!' he exclaimed, 'let us know more about your friend, let us see the disguised girl. After all now, we are sharers in the secret; we will promise, we will swear, but let us see the girl!'

'O, how he's on fire!' Philine cried, 'just be calm, just be patient, nothing is going to come of it today.'

'Then let us just have her name!' Wilhelm said.

'That would be a fine secret then,' Philine answered.

'At least just her Christian name.'

'If you can guess it, that's all right as far as I'm concerned. You can have three guesses, but no more; otherwise you could be taking me through the whole calendar.'

'Good,' said Wilhelm; 'is it Cecilia?'

'Nothing to do with Cecilia!'

'Henrietta?'

'Not at all! Watch out! Your curiosity will have to have a good night's rest!'

Wilhelm hesitated and trembled; he wanted to open his mouth, but speech deserted him. 'Mariane?' he eventually stammered, 'Mariane!'

'Bravo!' Philine exclaimed, 'that's it!', and as was her habit she turned round on her heel.

Wilhelm could not utter a word, and Serlo, who had not noticed how moved he was, continued to try to persuade Philine to open the door.

How surprised the two consequently were when Wilhelm all at once and with fervour interrupted their banter, threw himself down at Philine's feet and besought and implored her with the most vehement expression of passion. 'Let me see the girl,' he exlaimed, 'she's mine, it's my Mariane! She whom I have yearned for every day of my life, she who for me still comes before all other women in the world! At least go in to her, tell her that I'm here, the man who linked his first love and the entire happiness of his youth with her. He will be glad to explain why he left her in an unfriendly manner, he will beg her pardon, he will forgive her however she may have failed him, and he will even make no further claims upon her, if only he can see her once more, if only he can see that she is alive and happy!'

Philine shook her head and said: 'My friend, do talk quietly! Let us not deceive ourselves; and if the woman really is your friend, we must treat her with consideration, for in no way is she expecting to see you here. Quite different matters are what bring her here, and I'm sure you know that people would often rather see a ghost than an old lover at the wrong time. I will question her and prepare her, and we will consider what is to be done. I will write a note to you tomorrow, telling you when you are to come or whether you may come; obey me closely, for I vow that nobody shall set eyes on this dear creature against my will and the will of my friend. It is better that I keep my doors locked, and you won't want to seek me out with axe and hatchet.'

Wilhelm implored her, Serlo argued with her, but in vain. The two friends had to give way and depart from the room and the house.

Everyone can imagine what a restless night Wilhelm spent. It is understandable how slowly the hours of the day passed by while he was expecting Philine's note. Unfortunately he had to perform on that same evening; he had never suffered greater agony. After the play was over he hurried to Philine without in fact asking whether he was invited. He found her door locked, and the people in the building said that Mademoiselle had gone off early that day with a young officer; she had said that she would be coming back in a few days, it was true, but they did not believe it because she had paid up and taken her things with her.

Wilhelm was beside himself at this news. He hurried to Laertes and suggested to him that they should go after her and, whatever it might cost, obtain definite information about her companion. Laertes reproved his friend on account of his passion and credulity. 'I am willing to bet that it's none other than Friedrich,' he said. 'The boy is from a good family, I know this for sure; he is madly in love with the girl and has presumably wheedled so much money from his relatives that he can live with her again for a time.'

Wilhelm was not convinced by these remarks, but was none the less doubtful. Laertes explained to him how improbable the fairy-tale was that Philine had deluded them with, how very well figure and hair would fit in with Friedrich, that it would not be so easy to catch up with them as they had had twelve hours' start, and above all that Serlo could not do without either of them in the play.

With all these reasons Wilhelm was finally persuaded, though only to the extent that he gave up the idea of pursuing them himself. That same evening Laertes was able to procure a reliable man who could be given the task. He was a steady person who had served several noble families as courier and guide on journeys, and who happened to be without employment at this time. They gave him money and informed him about the whole business, presenting him with the task of seeking out the refugees and catching them up, of not then letting them out of his eyes, and of at once notifying the friends, wherever and however he might find them. He mounted horse that very hour and rode after the dubious couple, and to some extent at least Wilhelm was calmed by this measure.

Chapter Sixteen

Philine's departure caused no remarkable sensation, either in the theatre company or among the public. There was little seriousness in anything she undertook; women hated her as a rule, and men would have rather seen her in private than on the stage, and in this way her fine talent, which was an asset to the stage itself, was lost. The other members of the company took all the more trouble; Madame Melina in particular distinguished herself with assiduity and attentiveness. She observed Wilhelm's principles, adjusted herself to his theories and example, and from this time on had a certain something about her that made her more interesting. She soon achieved a true acting style, acquiring fully the natural conversational manner and succeeding to a limited extent with the emotional approach. She learnt how to fit into Serlo's moods and worked on her singing in order to please him, and she soon made as much progress with singing as is needful for social entertainment.

The company was made even more complete by some new actors who had been taken on, and while Wilhelm and Serlo each had influence in his own way, the former urging in every play towards the meaning and tone of the whole, the latter conscientiously going through the individual sections, the actors too were invigorated by praiseworthy zeal and the public took a lively interest in them.

'We are following a good path', Serlo said on one occasion, 'and if we continue like this, the public too will soon be on the right road. It is possible to confuse people very easily through crazy and unseemly performances; but if we lay before them what is sensible and proper, they are sure to aim for it.

'What is mainly lacking in our theatre and why neither actors nor audiences have the opportunity for reflection is that it really is too lively, and that there are no bounds where one could support one's judgment. It doesn't seem any advantage to me that we have, so to speak, extended our stage to an unending natural scene; but now neither theatre-director nor actors can withdraw to a constricted space, until such time as the taste of the nation perhaps indicates the right circle itself. Every good society exists only under certain conditions, and the same is true of a good theatre. Certain manners and ways of speech must be barred, as must certain objects and ways of behaving. One does not become poorer when one concentrates one's domestic concerns.'

They were more or less in agreement and not in agreement about this. Wilhelm and the majority were on the side of the English style of theatre, while Serlo and some others supported French theatre.

It was agreed that they should come together in their spare time (of which an actor unfortunately has so much), in order to go through the most famous plays of both types of theatre and to take note of what was best and worth imitating in them. Furthermore, a start was really made with some French plays. Aurelia went away every time the reading started. At first they thought that she was ill; on one occasion, however, Wilhelm, who had noticed what she was doing, asked her about it.

'I'm not going to be present when any such reading is taking place', she said, 'for how am I to hear and pass judgment, when my heart is broken? I hate the French language from the bottom of my heart.'

'How is it possible to be inimical to a language to which one owes the greatest part of one's education', Wilhelm exclaimed, 'and to which we must be even more indebted before our nature can attain a distinctive shape?'

'It is not a prejudice', Aurelia replied; 'an unfortunate impression, a hateful memory of my unfaithful friend has robbed me of any pleasure from this beautiful and cultivated language. How heartily I now dislike it! During the time of our friendly relationship he used to write German, and what a cordial, sincere and strong German it was! Now that he wanted to get rid of me, he began to write in French, something which had occasionally happened before only in fun. I felt and I noted what it was supposed to indicate. What he blushed to say in his mother-tongue, he could now write down with a good conscience. It is a first-rate language for reservations, half-measures and lies; it is a perfidious language! I can't find any German word, thank God, to express "perfidious" in its full compass. Our wretched "faithless" is an innocent child by comparison. Perfidious means unfaithful with pleasure, arrogance and malicious enjoyment. Oh, how enviable is the stage of development of a nation, which can express such fine nuances in one word! French is truly the language of the world, worthy of being the universal language, so that people can all just deceive and lie to each other! The letters he wrote in French were still agreeable enough to read. If you wanted to use your imagination, they sounded warm and even impassioned; but looked at closely, they were empty phrases, accursèd empty phrases! He has spoiled all my joy in the whole language, in French literature, even in the fine and choice expression of noble spirits in this tongue; I shudder when I hear a French word!'

She could continue for hours in this way to show her displeasure and to interrupt or upset any other conversation. Sooner or later Serlo would bring her peevish remarks to an end with a certain bitterness; but usually conversation had been destroyed for that evening.

On the whole it is unfortunately the case that nothing that is to be produced by the coming together of several people and circumstances can be maintained to perfection for a long period. The moment can usually be indicated, of a theatre company as well as of an empire, of a circle of friends as well as of an army, when these have been at the highest level of their perfection, harmony, contentment and activity; but often there is a rapid change of personnel, new people come along, the individuals no longer fit the circumstances, and the circumstances no longer fit the individuals, and what had previously been held together, now soon falls apart. Thus it could be said that Serlo's company was for a time as perfect as any German troupe could have prided itself on being. Most of the actors kept to their places; they all had enough to do, and all were glad to do what needed doing. Their personal relationships were tolerable, and each appeared to promise much in his art because he took the first steps with spirit and cheerfulness. However, it was soon evident that some of them were after all only automata who could merely attain to what could be reached without feeling, and soon there came the intervention of those passions which usually become an obstacle to any good arrangement and so easily pull apart all that sensible and right-thinking people wish to hold together.

Philine's departure was not so insignificant as had been believed at first. She had been able to keep Serlo entertained in a very adroit way and to stimulate the others more or less. She put up with Aurelia's vehemence with great patience, and it was her particular task to flatter Wilhelm. In these ways she was a kind of binding agent for the whole group, and her loss could not but be perceptible soon.

Serlo could not exist without being involved in some little love-affair. Elmira, who had grown up within a short time and, you could almost say, had become beautiful, had been attracting his attention for a long time now, and Philine was clever enough to aid and abet this passion, whose existence she had noticed. 'You have to get your hand in at match-making in good time,' she used to say; 'after all, there's nothing else left for us when we get old.' Consequently Serlo and Elmira had come closer to such an extent that after Philine had gone they soon came to an understanding, and the little romance intrigued them both all the more because they had every reason to keep it a secret from the Old Man who would not have made light of such an irregularity. Elmira's sister was in on the secret too, and in consequence Serlo had to overlook a great deal in both girls. One of their greatest shortcomings was an immoderate eating of sweets, indeed, if you like, an intolerable greediness, in which respect they by no means resembled Philine who acquired a new aura of amiability because she lived only on air, as it were, ate very little and merely sipped away at the bubbles of a glass of champagne with the greatest delicacy.

But now, if he wanted to please his beauty, he had to join breakfast with lunch and link the latter with dinner by means of afternoon tea. At the same time Serlo had a plan the execution of which was troubling him. He believed he could perceive a certain liking between Wilhelm and Aurelia, and wished very much that it would develop seriously. He hoped that he might burden Wilhelm with all the routine parts of theatre management and find in him, as he had done in his first brother-in-law, a faithful and industrious instrument. He had already gradually and imperceptibly passed over the greater part of the management to him, Aurelia looked after the box-office, and Serlo lived again just as he wanted to, as in earlier times. Yet there was something that secretly upset both him and his sister.

The public has a peculiar way of behaving towards public figures of acknowledged merit; it gradually begins to become indifferent towards them and favours talents that are far inferior but newly arrived; it makes exaggerated demands of the former and puts up with anything from the latter.

Serlo and Aurelia had opportunity enough to form their judgments about this. The new arrivals, particularly the young and handsome ones, had attracted all attention and applause to themselves, and brother and sister had to leave the stage after their most zealous efforts without hearing the welcome sound of clapping hands. Admittedly there were further special reasons as well. Aurelia's haughtiness was noticeable, and many were informed about her scorn for the audience. It was true, Serlo flattered everyone individually, but his sharp remarks about the generality were also often passed around and repeated. The new members of the cast on the other hand were partly strange and unknown, partly young, amiable and in need of help, and had therefore all acquired patrons as well.

There were also soon internal disturbances and various irritations; for no sooner had they noticed that Wilhelm had taken over the duties of a stage-manager than most of the actors began to become all the more awkward, when, in his own way, he wished to bring rather more order and precision into the whole and insisted in particular that each routine matter should be dealt with above all in a punctual and orderly fashion.

In a short while the whole relationship, which really had remained almost ideal for a time, had become as sordid as that in any itinerant theatre company. And unfortunately, at the very moment when Wilhelm had become acquainted by means of effort, industry and exertion with all the demands of the profession and had adapted his personality as well as his activity to these, it finally seemed in dark hours that his craft merited the necessary expenditure and the recompense of time and energy less than any other. The work was tiresome and the recompense slight. He felt that he would have rather undertaken any other occupation, where after all, when the work is done, one can enjoy quietness of mind, than this one, where, after overcoming efforts of a mechanical kind, one is to achieve through the greatest endeavours of mind and emotion the goal of one's activity. He had to listen to Aurelia's complaints about her brother's wastefulness, and he had to misunderstand Serlo's hints when the latter endeavoured to direct him from afar towards marriage with his sister. While doing so, he had to conceal the worry that was weighing upon him most heavily, as the messenger sent out after the ambivalent officer failed to return and did not send any messages, and consequently our friend was afraid he had lost his Mariane for a second time.

At the same time a period of public mourning occurred which meant that the theatre had to be closed for several weeks. He used this interlude in order to visit that clergyman in whose care the Harpist had been entrusted as a boarder. He found him in a pleasant location, and the first sight that caught his eye in the courtyard of the parsonage was the old man who was giving a boy a lesson on his instrument. He showed a great deal of pleasure in seeing Wilhelm again, stood up, proffered him his hand and said: 'You see that I am still useful for something in the world after all; allow me to continue, for the lessons are of limited time.'

The clergyman greeted Wilhelm in the most friendly manner and told him that the old man was already getting on quite well and that they hoped that he might make a complete recovery.

Their conversation naturally turned to the method of curing the insane.

'Apart from physical factors which often put insuperable difficulties in our way and about which I take the advice of a thoughtful doctor,' the clergyman said, 'I find that the means to heal insanity are very simple. They are precisely the same by which healthy people are prevented from becoming mad. If their spontaneous initiative is aroused, if they are made used to order, and if they are given the thought that they share their life and fate with so many others, and that extraordinary talent, the greatest happiness and the most intense misfortune are only slight deviations from what is usual, then no insanity will creep in, and if it is there, it will gradually disappear. I have given the old man a timetable, he teaches the harp to a few children, he helps with work in the garden and is already much more cheerful. He wants to enjoy eating the cabbage that he has planted, and to be really assiduous in giving lessons to my son, to whom he has bequeathed the harp in the eventuality of his own death, so that the boy will in fact be able to use the instrument. As clergyman I try to say only a little to him about his strange scruples, but an active life brings with it so many happenings that he must soon feel that every kind of doubt can only be removed by activity. I go to work gently; but if in addition I can get his beard and cowl off him, I shall have gained a great deal: for nothing brings us nearer to madness than when we make ourselves different from other people, and nothing preserves our normal sense so much as living in general accord with many people. How much therefore is there not unfortunately in our education and our civic institutions that causes us to prepare ourselves and our children for madness.'

Wilhelm remained for some days as guest of this sensible man and heard most interesting stories, not only concerning the insane but also of those who are usually considered prudent, indeed wise, and whose peculiarities come close to madness.

But the conversation became three times as lively when the doctor entered; he often used to visit his friend the clergyman and to support him in his humane endeavours. He was an oldish man who had spent many years in the practice of the noblest duties, though his health was poor. He was a great friend of country life and could hardly exist except in the open air; at the same time he was very gregarious and active, and for many years had had a particular inclination to be on friendly terms with all country clergymen. He tried to support in every possible way everyone whom he knew to be pursuing a useful occupation; he endeavoured to persuade others who were still undecided to take up a hobby; and as he was at the same time in touch with nobles, bailiffs and legal officials, he had been quietly contributing over a period of twenty years a great deal to the cultivation of many branches of agriculture and had been setting in motion everything that would be beneficial to the land, the animals and human beings, thus encouraging the truest form of enlightenment. He said that for anyone it was a misfortune if there became fixed in his mind some idea or other which had no influence on active life or indeed even withdrew him from active life. 'I have at present a case of this kind', he said, 'with a fashionable and wealthy couple on whose behalf up to now all skill has been spent in vain; the case almost belongs to your department, my dear Pastor, and this young man will not spread the story any further.

'During a distinguished man's absence a young person was dressed up in this gentleman's indoor clothing, as a not wholly creditable practical joke. His wife was to be taken in by this, and although the incident was only told me as a piece of foolery, I am very much afraid that there was the intention of leading this excellent and amiable lady away from the proper path. The husband comes back unexpectedly, goes into his own room, believes that he is seeing himself, and from that time onwards takes on a mood of melancholy in which he develops the conviction that he will die soon.

'He is giving himself up to people who flatter him with religious notions, and I don't see how he is to be prevented from joining the Moravian Brethren along with his wife and, as he has no children, from depriving his relatives of the major part of his wealth.'

'With his wife?' Wilhelm exclaimed vehemently, for this story had startled him not a little.

'And unfortunately,' added the doctor, who believed he could detect in Wilhelm's exclamation no more than philanthropic sympathy, 'this lady has been subjected to an even deeper anxiety which causes her to feel that withdrawal from the world would not be repugnant. This very young man is saying goodbye to her, she is not careful enough to conceal a budding inclination; he becomes bold, embraces her and in so doing presses the large-sized miniature portrait of her husband, studded with brilliants as it is, violently against her breast. She feels an intense pain, which gradually disperses, leaving at first a small red mark and then no trace at all. As a human being I am convinced that she has nothing further to reproach herself with; as a doctor I am sure that this pressure will have no bad after-effects, but she refuses to give up the idea that there is an induration there, and when the attempt is made to remove the delusion from her through feeling, she maintains that it is only at this moment that there is nothing to feel; she firmly imagines that this trouble will end with a cancerous sore, and that in this way her youth and charm will be completely lost for herself and for others.'

'What an unhappy wretch I am!' Wilhelm cried, striking his forehead and rushing away from the company into the open. Never before had he been in such a state.

The doctor and the clergyman, highly surprised at this strange revelation, had their hands full with him in the evening when he came back and reproached himself most bitterly while making a more complete confession in connection with this incident. Both men were most sympathetic with him, especially as he now told them about the rest of his situation, using, what is more, the black colouring of his mood at that moment.

Next day the doctor did not delay in agreeing to go with him to the town and to keep him company, in order to procure help, where this was possible, for Aurelia whom her friend had left behind in dubious circumstances.

These were in fact worse than they had surmised. She had a kind of intermittent fever, which was all the less manageable since she deliberately supported and aggravated the attacks in her own way. The stranger was not introduced as a doctor and behaved in a very agreeable and sensible manner. There was talk about the condition of her body and her mind, and the new friend told a number of stories to show how people can live to a ripe old age in spite of a sickliness of this kind; but nothing was more harmful in such cases, he said, than a deliberate renewal of passionate feelings. In particular he did not hide the fact that he had found those people very fortunate who had been destined, in cases when their disposition to poor health could not be fully cured, to nurture truly religious convictions within themselves. He said this in a very modest way, and as it were historically, while promising to provide his new friends some very interesting reading material in a manuscript that he had received from the hands of an admirable lady who had been his friend and who had since then died. 'It is infinitely valuable to me,' he said, 'and I am entrusting you with the original itself. Only the title is mine: "Confessions of a beautiful soul".'

The doctor further gave Wilhelm his best advice concerning the dietetic and medicinal treatment of the unfortunate, highly strung Aurelia, promising to write and if possible to come again in person.

In the meantime a change had been prepared in Wilhelm's absence which he could not have anticipated. During his administration Wilhelm had treated the whole business with a certain freedom and liberality, had looked to things very well, and especially with costumes, decorations and properties had acquired everything in an ample and decent style; what is more, in order to retain people's good will he had flattered their self-interest, since he could not make an impression on them by means of nobler motives; and in this respect he saw himself as all the more justified because Serlo himself did not claim to be a precise manager; he liked to hear praise of his theatre's splendour and was contented if Aurelia, who looked after all the housekeeping, could assure him that she had no debts, once all expenses had been defrayed, and could furthermore provide as much as was necessary to pay the debts which Serlo might have incurred meanwhile in his unusual generosity to his lady-friends and in other ways.

Melina, who had meanwhile been looking after the wardrobe, had been watching the situation, cold and malicious as he was, and knew how to make Serlo aware, while Wilhelm was away and with the increasing illness of Aurelia, that they could in fact increase the takings, spend less and either save up some money or else in the last resort live more merrily as they pleased. Serlo was glad to hear this, and Melina ventured to put his plan forward.

'I don't want to maintain that any one of the actors is at present being overpaid,' he said: 'they are worthy people, and they would be welcome anywhere; but bearing in mind the income they provide us, they do receive too much. My proposal would be to make arrangements for an opera, and as far as drama is concerned, I must tell you that you are the man who can provide a whole drama on his own. Don't you have to experience at this moment how your merits are not properly recognized? It is not because your fellow-actors are first-rate, but because they are good that your extraordinary talents no longer receive due acclaim.

'Just present yourself alone, as must have happened before, attempt to attract mediocre, indeed I may say poor people at a low wage, put them into shape, as you know how so well, as far as routine factors are concerned, use the rest for the opera, and you will see that with the same effort and the same cost you will cause more pleasure and will earn much more money than hitherto.'

Serlo was too flattered for his objections to have any force. He gladly conceded to Melina that with his interest in music he had long wished for something of the sort; but at the same time he expressed his awareness that the inclinations of the public would thereby be led even further down wrong paths, and with such a mixture of a theatre that was neither proper opera nor proper drama, what was left as far as the appreciation of a definite and full approach to a work of art was concerned would of necessity be completely lost.

Melina made fun in a not entirely refined way of Wilhelm's pedantic ideals in this direction, and of the presumption in educating the public instead of letting oneself be educated by it, and both agreed with great conviction that it was only a matter of taking in money, becoming rich or having a good time, and scarcely concealed their wish to be rid only of those people who stood in the way of their plan. Melina expressed his regret that Aurelia's poor health could not promise her long life, but he thought precisely the opposite. Serlo seemed to be complaining that Wilhelm was not a singer, and intimated thereby that he believed he could soon be dispensed with. Melina came forward with a whole list of savings that could be made, and Serlo saw him as the threefold replacement of his first brother-in-law. They felt certainly that they had to keep secret the subject of this conversation, but were in consequence even more closely linked to one another and took opportunities to have secret discussions about everything that had happened, to find fault with whatever Aurelia and Wilhelm undertook and to work out their new project in their thoughts more and more.

However quiet they both might be about their plan and however little they might betray themselves by words, they were not politic enough to conceal their views in their behaviour. Melina opposed Wilhelm in many instances which were in the latter's field, and Serlo, who had never dealt gently with his sister, only became more bitter, the more her ill-health increased, and the more she would have deserved consideration on account of her unstable and passionate moods.

It was at this very time that *Emilia Galotti* was being performed. The casting of this play fitted in felicitously, and everyone could demonstrate the whole range of their acting within the limited scope of this tragedy. As Marinelli Serlo was in his element, Odoardo's role was very well delivered, Madame Melina played the part of the mother with much insight, Elmira showed herself to advantage in the role of Emilia, Laertes appeared with much dignity as Appiani, and Wilhelm had devoted several months' study to the part of the Prince. In so doing he had often discussed, both with himself and with Serlo and Aurelia, the question of whether a distinction can be made between noble and elegant behaviour and to what extent the former quality needs to be contained in the latter, but the latter quality is not necessarily contained in the former.

Serlo, who as Marinelli presented the courtier straight, without elements of caricature, had a number of good ideas on this subject. 'Elegant dignity,' he said, 'is difficult to imitate because it is in fact negative and assumes long, continuous practice. For in one's behaviour, for instance, one should not depict something that declares itself as dignity; rather, you should avoid all that is unworthy and common; you should never forget always to pay attention to yourself and to others, not to let yourself down, to do not too little and not too much for other people, to seem stirred by nothing and moved by nothing, never to be in too much of a hurry, to be able to be composed at all times, and in this way to attain to an outward balance, even if inwardly it may be as stormy as it will. A noble man can be negligent about himself at times, an elegant man never. The latter is like a very well-dressed man; he will never lean against anything, and everybody will be on guard against touching him; he is distinguished from others, and yet he may not stand alone; for as in every art, so too in this one, whatever is most difficult in the last resort is to be executed with ease; thus the elegant man, in spite of all separation, should always seem to be linked with others, he should on no occasion be stiff, he should everywhere be skilful, always appear first and yet never press importunately as such.

'So you can see that in order to appear as elegant, you really have to be elegant, one can see why on the average women can give themselves the air of being thus more than men can, and why courtiers and soldiers approach this dignity most quickly.'

Wilhelm almost despaired now about his part, but Serlo came to his aid again by presenting to him the subtlest of observations about details and by fitting him out in such a way that during the performance he portrayed a really fine prince, at least in the eyes of the crowd.

Serlo had promised to let him have after the performance the comments which he would in any case be making about him; but an unpleasant quarrel between brother and sister prevented any critical discussion. Aurelia had played the part of Orsina in a manner that will probably never be seen again. Altogether she was very familiar with the part and had handled it in a perfunctory way during the rehearsals; at the perfomance itself, however, she opened up all the sluice-gates of her personal distress, as one might say, and the result was a presentation of a type that no poet in the first flights of fantasy could have imagined. Stormy applause from the audience rewarded her pain-ridden efforts, but when people went to her after the performance she was lying half-unconscious in a chair.

Serlo had already expressed his irritation at what he called her exaggerated style of acting and at the exposure of her innermost heart to the audience who were after all more or less familiar with that unfortunate story, and as he was accustomed to doing when he was angry, he had been grinding his teeth and stamping his feet. 'Leave her alone,' he said when he discovered her in the chair surrounded by the others, 'very soon she will appear stark naked on the stage, and then for the first time the applause will be really perfect.'

'You ungrateful and inhumane wretch!' she cried out. 'I shall soon be carried naked to that place where no applause reaches our ears any more!' With these words she leapt up and hurried to the door. The maid had neglected to bring her her coat, the sedan chair was not there; it had been raining, and a very cold wind was blowing through the streets. It was in vain that people pleaded with her, for she was excessively heated; she deliberately walked slowly and praised the coolness which she seemed to be breathing in really avidly. She was scarcely at home when she could hardly utter a word for hoarseness; but she did not admit that she felt completely stiff in her neck and down her back. It was not long before she was afflicted by a paralysis of the tongue, so that she was speaking one word instead of another; she was put to bed, and by the frequent application of expedients one ailment was assuaged, while another one showed itself. The fever became intense and her condition dangerous.

During the next morning she had a quiet hour. She asked for Wilhelm and handed him a letter. 'This note,' she said, 'has already been waiting a long time for this moment. I feel that the end of my life is approaching soon; promise me that you will deliver it in person and that you will avenge with a few words my sufferings from the unfaithful man. He is not without feeling, and my death at least should grieve him for a short time.'

Wilhelm took the letter, consoling her none the less and trying to remove the thought of death from her mind.

'No,' she rejoined, 'don't deprive me of the hope that is nearest to me. I have long expected death and will embrace it joyfully.'

Shortly afterwards the manuscript promised by the doctor arrived. She begged Wilhelm to read to her from the manuscript, and the reader will best be able to judge the effect it had when he has become acquainted with the Book that follows. The impetuous and defiant character of our poor friend was all at once soothed. She took the letter back and wrote another, as it seemed, in a very gentle mood; she also requested Wilhelm to console her friend, if he should be in any way dispirited by the news of her death, and to assure him that she had forgiven him and that she wished him every happiness.

From this time onwards she was very quiet and seemed to occupy herself only with a few ideas which she endeavoured to acquire from the manuscript, out of which Wilhelm had to read to her from time to time. The decline in her strength was not perceptible, and one morning unexpectedly Wilhelm found her dead, when he was going to visit her.

With the respect in which he had held her and accustomed as he was to having her company, her loss was very grievous to him. She was the only person who really meant well towards him, and recently he had been all too aware of Serlo's coldness. He, therefore, made haste to carry out the task that had been entrusted to him, and wished to go away for some time. On the other hand this departure was very welcome to Melina: for in the course of the extensive correspondence that he kept up, he had been negotiating at once with a male and a female singer, who in due course were to prepare the audiences through intermezzi for the opera that was to come. The loss of Aurelia and Wilhelm's departure were to be borne in the first period in this way, and our friend was content with anything that would make his leave of absence for some weeks easier.

He had made out his task to himself as a particularly important idea. The death of his friend had moved him deeply and as he had witnessed her so early departure from the scene, he could not help being inimically disposed to the man who had cut her life short and made this short life so painful for her.

Notwithstanding the last, gentle words of the dying woman, he resolved to pass stern judgment on the unfaithful friend when handing over the letter, and as he was reluctant to trust the mood of the moment, he thought of a speech which, as it worked out, became more emotionally charged than was reasonable. After he had fully convinced himself of the good composition of his essay, he learnt it off by heart and made preparations for his departure. Mignon was with him as he was packing, and asked him whether he was going southwards or northwards, and when she heard from him that he was to travel in the latter direction, she said: 'In that case I will expect you here again.' She asked him if she could have Mariane's pearl necklace, and this he could not refuse the dear creature; she already had the scarf. In return she put the Ghost's veil into his portmanteau, although he told her that this gauze would be of no use to him.

Melina took over the management, and his wife promised to keep a motherly eye on the children, from whom Wilhelm was loath to be separated. Felix was in a very merry mood at the parting, and when he was asked what he would like to have brought back to him as a present, he said: 'Listen! Bring me a father.' Mignon took Wilhelm's hand as he was parting, and standing on tiptoe she gave him a true-hearted and vigorous kiss on the lips, though without any caressing endearment, saying: 'Master, don't forget us and come back soon.'

And so we let our friend set off on his journey amid a thousand thoughts and feelings, and further record here finally a poem that Mignon had recited a number of times with great expression and that we were prevented from communicating earlier by the pressure of so many strange events.

> Ask me not to speak, but leave me silent,
> For my secret is a duty for me;
> I'd like to show you all my inner being,
> But such is not the Fates' decree.

> When the time is right the sun's course drives away
> The sombre night, and daylight starts to glow,
> The hard rock gladly opens up its heart,
> And gives to earth the springs concealed below.

> Each one seeks peace and calm in his friend's arms,
> For here the heart's laments can be expressed;
> And yet my lips, which are locked fast by an oath,
> Can only be unsealed at a god's behest.

BOOK SIX

Confessions of a Beautiful Soul

Until my eighth year I was a completely healthy child, but I can remember as little about this time as about the day of my birth. I had a haemorrhage at the start of my eighth year, and at that moment my personality became all sensibility and memory. The most trivial details of this occurrence are still in my mind's eye, as if it had happened yesterday.

During the nine months that I was confined to bed, a period which I endured with patience, the basis of my whole way of thinking was laid, as it seems to me, in that the first resources were offered to my mind to enable it to develop in its own way.

I suffered and loved; this was in fact the shape of my heart. In the midst of the most violent attack of coughing and during a wearying fever I was as quiet as a snail which withdraws into its shell; as soon as I had a little air I desired to experience something pleasant, and as all other pleasure was denied me, I endeavoured to compensate myself through my eyes and ears. I was brought dolls and picture-books, and whoever wanted to sit by my bedside had to tell me a story.

I gladly heard Bible stories from my mother; Father entertained me with natural objects. He possessed a good collection. Every now and again he brought one drawer after the other down, showed me the things and gave me truthful explanations of them. Dried plants and insects and various kinds of anatomical preparations, human skin, bones, mummies and the like found their way to the little girl's sickbed; birds and animals that he had killed while hunting were shown to me before they went to the kitchen; and in order that the prince of this world too should have a voice in this assembly, my aunt told me love stories and fairytales. Everything was accepted, and everything took root. There were hours when I conversed in lively manner with the invisible being; I can still recall a few lines of verse which my mother wrote down as I dictated them.

Frequently I related back to my father what I had learnt from him. It was not easy for me to take some medicine without asking where the things grew which it was made from, what they looked like, and what they were called. But my aunt's stories had also not fallen on stony ground. I thought of myself in beautiful clothes encountering the most delightful princes who could not rest until they knew who the unknown beauty was. I continued such a long time in a similar adventure with a charming little angel who in white robe and with golden wings was very much concerned about me that my imagination heightened the angelic image until it almost appeared.

After a year I had recovered fairly well; but nothing of a wild kind had been left with me from my early childhood. I could not even play with dolls, I desired things that would requite my love. I had much pleasure from dogs, cats and birds (my father kept all kinds of these); but what would I not have given to possess a creature that played a very important part in one of my aunt's fairytales. It was a lamb which had been caught and fed by a peasant girl in the forest, but within this amiable animal was a bewitched prince who in the end revealed himself as a handsome young man and rewarded his benefactress with his hand. Only too gladly would I have been the owner of a lamb like that!

But none was to be found now, and as everything around me took place with such complete naturalness, the hope of possessing anything so wonderful could not help almost disappearing in time. Meanwhile I consoled myself by reading books in which wondrous events were described. Among all these I was most fond of the *Christian German Hercules*[1]; the devout love-story was entirely according to my taste. If anything happened to his Valisca, and frightful things did happen to her, he prayed first before going to rescue her, and the prayers were given in full in the book. How much I liked that! My inclination to the invisible, which I was always obscurely aware of, was only enhanced in this way; for once and for all God too was to be my close friend.

As I went on growing, I read heaven knows what, all in confusion; but the *Roman Octavia*[2] was prized before all else. The persecutions of the early Christians, clothed in novel form, aroused in me a very lively interest.

Now Mother began to grumble about the continual reading; in order to please her, Father took the books from me one day, but he gave them back the next. She was sensible enough to notice that there was nothing to be done in this direction, and she only

1. Andreas Heinrich Buchholz, *Des christlichen Teutschen Grossfürsten Herkules und der böhmischen königlichen Fräulein Valisca Wundergeschichte*, 1669.
2. Anton Ulrich von Braunschweig, *Römische Octavia*, 1667. (Tr.)

insisted that the Bible too should be read equally diligently. In this respect too I did not need to be driven, and I read the sacred books with much sympathetic interest. At the same time my mother was always careful that no seductive books should come into my hands, and I myself would have cast aside any shameful piece of writing; for my princes and princesses were all extremely virtuous, and incidentally I knew more about the natural history of the human race than I let people see, and had learnt it mostly from the Bible. I brought together doubtful passages with words and things that I had directly encountered, and with my eagerness for knowledge and my powers of deduction I successfully found out the truth. If I had heard about witches, I should have also had to be introduced to witchcraft.

It was due to my mother and to this thirst for knowledge that for all my passionate attachment to books I did learn how to cook; but there was something to be seen in this process. To cut up a bird or a young pig was a festive occasion to me. I brought the entrails to Father, and he talked to me about them as if to a young student, and with heartfelt joy often referred to me as his failed son.

Now my twelfth year had been completed. I learnt French, dancing and drawing, and received the usual religious instruction. With this last many feelings and thoughts became active, but nothing that might have related to my own condition. I was glad to hear talk of God, and I was proud to be able to talk better about Him than others of my age; I now eagerly read a number of books that put me in the position of being able to chatter about religion, but it never occurred to me to think how things might be as far as I was concerned, whether my soul too was of such a quality, whether it resembled a mirror from which the eternal sun could be reflected; I had already assumed that once and for all.

I learnt French with great eagerness. My language teacher was a good sound man. He was not a frivolous empiricist nor a dry grammarian; he was a man of knowledge, he had seen the world. Along with the language tuition he satisfied my desire for knowledge in various ways. I was so very fond of him that I always used to await his arrival with a beating heart. Drawing was not difficult for me, and I should have made better progress if my teacher of drawing had had intelligence and knowledge; but all he had was dexterity and practice.

At first dancing was only my slightest pleasure; my body was too sensitive, and I only learnt in my sister's company. However, because of our dancing-master's idea of giving a ball to all his pupils, my enjoyment of this exercise came to life quite differently.

Among a lot of boys and girls two sons of the court marshall
were outstanding: the younger was as old as I was, the other one
two years older, children of such beauty that according to general
consent they surpassed anything in the way of beautiful children
that had ever been seen. As soon as I too had seen them, I took
notice of no one else from the whole crowd. At that moment I
danced attentively and wished to dance beautifully. How did it
happen that these boys too noticed me in preference to all
others?—Enough; in the first hour we were the best of friends,
and before the little entertainment had come to an end, we had
already arranged where we would meet again very soon. This was
a great joy for me. But I was most delighted when they both next
morning inquired after me, each in a gallant note that was
accompanied by a bunch of flowers. Never again was I to feel the
way I did then! Compliments were repaid by compliments, little
letters by little letters. From now on church-going and taking
walks were opportunities for rendezvous; our young friends
always invited us together, but we were clever enough to conceal
the affair in such a way that our parents had no more knowledge
of it than we thought good.

I had now obtained two lovers at once. I had not decided for
either one of them. I liked them both, and we were on the best of
terms. Suddenly the elder boy was very ill; I myself had already
often been very ill and knew how to give pleasure to the patient by
conveying many courtesies to him and by sending him delicacies
that would be appropriate to a sick person, so that his parents
gratefully acknowledged the attention, listened to their dear son's
request and invited me together with my sisters to visit him as
soon as ever he had ceased to be confined to his bed. The
tenderness with which he received me was not childish, and from
that day on I had chosen him. He warned me straightaway to keep
the matter secret from his brother; but the fire could no longer be
hidden, and the younger brother's jealousy made it a complete
romance. He played us a thousand tricks; he took pleasure in
destroying our happiness and thereby augmented the passion
which he was attempting to destroy.

Now I really had found the lamb I had wished for, and this
passion, like some other illness, had the effect of making me quiet
and of withdrawing me from lively pleasures. I was solitary and
sensitive, and I thought of God again. He remained my close
friend, and I well remember with what tears I persevered in
praying for the boy, who continued to be ill.

Although there was much that was childish in the process, it
contributed much to the development of my heart. Instead of the

usual translation we had to write every day to our French
language teacher letters of our own invention. I put my own love
story on the market under the name of Phyllis and Damon. The
old man soon saw what it was about, and in order to make me
trusting, he praised my work very highly. I became even bolder,
opened out candidly and was faithful to the truth down to details.
I no longer recall in what context he once took the opportunity to
say: 'How agreeable, how natural it is! But the good Phyllis had
better be careful, it may soon become serious.'

I was annoyed that he did not already consider the matter a
serious one, and I asked him in an offended manner what he
understood by serious. He did not wait to be asked a second time
and explained himself so clearly that I could scarcely conceal my
fright. But as I immediately afterwards felt a mood of irritation
and took it amiss that he could think such thoughts, I pulled
myself together, wished to defend my heroine and said with cheeks
as red as fire: 'But, sir, Phyllis is a respectable girl!'

At that he was malicious enough to make fun of me with my
respectable heroine and, as we were speaking French, to play with
the word *honnête* in order to take Phyllis' respectability through
all the meanings. I felt the ridiculous side of this and became very
confused. He broke off, not wanting to make me timid, but on
other occasions brought the conversation round to this subject
again. Plays and little stories which I read and translated with
him, often gave him cause to show what a weak protection so-
called virtue is against the demands of strong feeling. I gave up
arguing, but was always secretly annoyed, and his comments
became a burden to me.

I also gradually lost all contact with my good Damon. The
intrigues of the younger brother had caused our association to
break up. Not long after both boys died in the flower of their
youth. This distressed me, but they were soon forgotten.

Now Phyllis grew up quickly, was in good health and began to
look around in society. The heir to the ruling prince married, and
a little later, after his father's death, commenced his reign. Court
and city were full of life and movement. Now there was plenty for
my curiosity to feed on. Now there were plays, balls and what goes
with these, and although our parents held us back as much as
possible, it was necessary all the same to appear at court where I
had been presented. There was an influx of foreigners, great social
events were taking place in all houses, some gentlemen had been
recommended to ourselves and others introduced, and at my
uncle's house people of all nations could be encountered.

My honest mentor continued to warn me in a discreet but

telling way, and I always secretly resented this. I was by no means convinced of the truth of this contention, and perhaps even at that time I was right, perhaps he was wrong, in believing women to be so weak in all circumstances; but at the same time he spoke so insistently that on one occasion I became anxious lest he might be right, and then said to him very spiritedly: 'As the danger is so great and the human heart so weak, I will ask God to look after me.'

The naive answer seemed to please him, he praised my intention; but within myself it was meant anything but seriously; this time it was only an empty phrase: for feelings for the Invisible One were almost extinguished within me. The crowd that surrounded me were a distraction to me and drew me along like a strong current. These were the emptiest years of my life. To talk about nothing for days together, to be without a single healthy thought and only to have impulsive enthusiasms—this was my lot. There was not even a thought for the books that had been so loved. The people around me had no inkling of intellectual matters; they were German courtiers, and this class of people had not the slightest culture in those days.

Such acquaintances, it might be thought, could not but lead me to the verge of perdition. I drifted along in sensuous cheerfulness, I did not compose myself, I did not pray, I thought neither of myself nor of God; but I see it as providential guidance that I was not attracted to any of the many handsome, rich and well-dressed men. They were dissolute and did not conceal the fact, and this frightened me off; they adorned their conversations with suggestive remarks, and this offended me, so that I behaved coldly towards them; their unseemliness passed all belief at times, and I allowed myself to be uncivil.

Moreover, my tutor had once revealed to me in confidence that as far as most of these wretched fellows were concerned not only the virtue but also the health of a girl were in danger. Now I really did have a horror of them, and I was already anxious when one of them came in any way too close to me. I was on my guard against glasses and cups, as also against a chair that one of the men had been sitting in. In this way I was morally and physically very isolated, and all the compliments they paid I proudly accepted as due to me like incense.

Among the friends who were in our circle at that time there stood out particularly a young man whom we jokingly called Narcissus. He had won a good name for himself in the diplomatic career and hoped to obtain a good position in the course of various changes that were taking place at our new court. He soon became acquainted with my father, and his knowledge and behaviour opened the door for him to a private circle of the best men. My father spoke very highly of him, and his handsome appearance would have made an even greater impression if his whole personality had not displayed a sort of complacency. I had seen and thought well of him, but we had never spoken to one another.

At a great ball, where he was also present, we danced a minuet together; this too did not lead to closer acquaintance. When the strenuous dances started, which I made a habit of avoiding for the sake of my father who was concerned for my health, I went into an adjoining room and conversed with older women friends who had sat down to play cards.

Narcissus, who had been leaping around with the others for some time, also came into the room where I was, and began to talk to me about various things, after he had recovered from a nose-bleeding that had befallen him while dancing. Within half an hour the conversation had become so interesting, although there was no trace of tenderness in it, that neither of us could think of dancing any longer. We were soon teased about it, without letting ourselves be confused by this. The next evening we could take up our conversation again, and we thus took good care of our health.

Now the acquaintance had been made. Narcissus paid his respects to me and my sisters, and now for the first time I began to realize again the things I knew, what I had thought of, what I had felt, and what I was able to talk about in conversation. My new friend, who had always been in the best society, had, in addition to the historical and political field that he knew well, very extensive literary knowledge, and he remained ignorant of nothing new, especially of what came out in France. He brought for me and sent to me many a pleasant book, but that had to be kept more secret than a forbidden understanding in love. Women of learning had been made fun of, and even those with some education were not to be tolerated, presumably because it was considered impolite to put so many ignorant men to shame. Even my father, to whom this new opportunity of developing my mind was very welcome, expressly required that this literary pursuit should remain a secret.

In this way our association went on almost a year and a day, as it were, and I could not say that Narcissus had in any way offered expressions of love or tenderness to me. He remained well-mannered and obliging, but showed no passion; indeed the charms of my youngest sister who was extremely beautiful at that time did not seem to be indifferent to him. He gave her in fun all sorts of friendly names from foreign languages, of which he spoke several very well, and from which he liked to introduce particular idioms into German conversation. She did not respond particularly to his compliments; she was bound by another tie, and as she was altogether very hasty and he was sensitive, they disagreed not infrequently about trivialities. He knew how to keep on good terms with Mother and the aunts, and thus he had gradually become a member of the family.

Who knows how much longer we would have gone on living in this way, if our circumstances had not been changed all at once by a strange chance. With my sisters I was invited to a certain house which I was not fond of visiting. The company was too mixed, and often people could be found there who were of the silliest, if not the most vulgar kind. On this occasion Narcissus had also been invited, and I was disposed to go for his sake: for, after all, I was sure to find somebody with whom I could converse in my own way. Already at the dining table we had to put up with quite a lot, for some men had been drinking heavily; after dinner we were to play forfeits, indeed we had to. The game was played in a very noisy and lively style. Narcissus had to redeem a pledge; he was required to whisper into everyone's ear something that would be agreeable to the whole company. He may have lingered too long by my neighbour, the wife of a captain. All at once the latter gave him a box on the ear which, as I was sitting quite close by, made the powder fly into my eyes. When I had wiped my eyes and to some extent recovered from the fright, I saw both men with naked daggers. Narcissus was bleeding, and the other man, beside himself with wine, anger and jealousy, could scarcely be restrained by all the rest of the party. I took Narcissus by the arm and led him out by the door and up a flight of stairs into another room, and, not thinking my friend safe from his mad opponent, I at once bolted the door.

Neither of us took the wound to be serious, for we only saw a slight slash on the hand; but soon we became aware of a stream of blood running down his back, and a large head-wound was revealed. Now I became anxious. I hurried to the landing to send for help, but could not see anybody, for everyone had stayed below in order to restrain the frantic fellow. At last a daughter of the house came up, and her cheerfulness caused me not a little anxiety since she was in the mood to split her sides laughing at the crazy uproar and the confounded comedy. I implored her urgently to find me a surgeon, and in her wild way she immediately dashed down the stairs in order to fetch one herself.

I returned to my wounded friend, bound his hand with my handkerchief and his head with a towel that was hanging on the door. He was still bleeding profusely: the wounded man turned pale and seemed to faint. There was nobody nearby who could have helped me; I took him into my arms in a very unconstrained manner and tried to encourage him by stroking and coaxing; he remained conscious, but sat there as pale as death.

Now at last the busy lady of the house came, and how shocked she was to see our friend lying in my arms in this condition and both of us covered with blood: for nobody had imagined that Narcissus was wounded; everybody thought that I had happily brought him out.

Now there was a superfluity of wine, perfumed water and whatever could be invigorating and refreshing, now too the surgeon came, and I could no doubt have left at this point; but Narcissus held firmly on to my hand, and I should have stayed still without being held. While he was being bandaged I continued to paint his skin with wine, counting it for little that the whole company was now standing about. The surgeon had ended, the wounded man took leave of me silently and with courtesy, and was carried home.

Now the lady of the house led me to her bedroom; she had to undress me completely, and I may not pass over in silence that, while his blood was being washed from my body, I became aware for the first time by chance in the mirror that I could consider myself as beautiful even without any covering. I could not put on any of my articles of clothing again, and as the people living in the house were all smaller or less slim than myself, I arrived home in a strange disguise, to the great surprise of my parents. They were extremely annoyed at my fright, at the wounds of our friend, at the captain's nonsense and about the whole incident. My father came very near to challenging the captain, in order to avenge his friend there and then. He upbraided the gentlemen present that they had not taken action against such treacherous behaviour at once; for it was only too obvious that after striking Narcissus, the captain had immediately taken out a dagger and wounded him from behind; the blow across the hand had just been delivered when Narcissus himself drew his dagger. I was indescribably upset and aroused, or how shall I put it; the emotion that was slumbering at the deepest level of my heart had suddenly broken loose, like a flame that finds air. And if pleasure and happiness are very skilful, so that they can first bring forth love and nurture it quietly, it will be most easily impelled by fright to make up its mind and declare itself, since it is by nature courageous. The little daughter was given medicine and put to bed. Early next morning my father hurried to our injured friend who lay seriously ill with a high temperature caused by the wound.

My father did not tell me much about what he had discussed with him and tried to set my mind at rest concerning the consequences which this incident might have. It was a question of whether one could be satisfied with an apology, or whether the matter had to go to law, and other comparable matters. I knew my father too well to believe that he wished to see this affair concluded without a duel; but I kept quiet, for I had learnt from my father at an early age that women were not to meddle in such quarrels. What is more, it did not seem as if anything had occurred between the two friends which would have concerned myself; but my father soon confided the content of his further talk with my mother. He had said that Narcissus had been extremely moved by the support I had provided, had embraced him, declared himself to be eternally indebted to me, and had indicated that he desired no happiness unless he could share it with me; he had asked to be allowed to regard him as a father. Mama faithfully reported all this to me, but did add the well-meant reminder that one should not pay all that much attention to something that had been said in a first flush of emotion. 'Yes, of course,' I replied with assumed coldness, feeling heaven knows what as I said it.

Narcissus was ill for two months and because of the wound on his right hand could not even write, but in the meantime showed his thoughts of me through most courteous attentions. All these more than usual civilities I compared with what I had heard from my mother, and my head was continually full of capricious thoughts. The whole town was talking about the incident. People talked to me about it in a special tone of voice and drew conclusions which always affected me very deeply, however much I tried to reject them. What hitherto had been dalliance and usage now became a matter of seriousness and real inclination. The agitation which I felt became all the more violent the more carefully I tried to hide it from everybody. The thought of losing him terrified me, and the possibility of a closer bond made me tremble. For a not too sensible girl the prospect of the married state indeed does have something terrifying about it.

These violent shocks recalled me to myself. All at once the pretty pictures of a life of distraction which up to now had been before my mind's eye night and day were swept away. My soul began to stir once more; but the acquaintance, which had been so interrupted, with the invisible Friend could not be resumed all that easily. We still remained at some distance from one another; there was some kind of relationship again, but as compared with other times a great difference.

A duel in which the captain was seriously wounded had taken

place without my hearing about it, and public opinion was
completely on the side of my beloved who at last appeared in
public again. In particular he arranged to be carried into our
house with his head and his hand in bandages. How my heart was
beating during this visit! The whole family was present; on both
sides conversation was limited to general expressions of gratitude
and courtesies; but he found an opportunity to convey to me some
secret indications of his tender feeling, in consequence of which
my agitation became only too marked. After he had fully
recovered, he visited us all through the winter on the same footing
as previously, and for all the gentle intimations of feeling and love
which he gave me, there was no discussion of anything.

In this way I was kept in constant training. There was no
human being in whom I could confide, and I was too remote from
God. In the course of four hectic years I had forgotten Him
completely; now I thought of Him occasionally again, but the
acquaintance had become cold. I only paid Him ceremonial visits,
and as furthermore I always put on fine clothes when I appeared
before Him and indicated to Him with satisfaction my virtue,
honesty and the advantages which I believed I had in preference
to other people, in all the finery He did not seem to notice me.

If his prince, from whom a courtier expects his fortune, were to
behave towards him in this way, the courtier would be very
disturbed; but I did not feel badly about this. I had what I needed,
health and comfort; if God wished to take pleasure at my
recollection of Him, all well and good; if not, I none the less
believed that I had done my duty.

It is true, I did not think like that of myself at the time; but this
was the true shape of my soul. But already preparations were in
hand to change and purify my attitude.

Spring came, and Narcissus visited me without prior notice at a
time when I was entirely on my own at home. Now he appeared as
a lover and asked me if I would give him my heart and, if he
should receive an honourable, well paid post, in due course my
hand.

Certainly, he had been admitted to our state service; but at first
he was held back rather than given rapid promotion, because
people were afraid of his ambition, and was kept at a small salary
because he had some private income.

For all my fondness of him, I knew that he was not the man
with whom one could deal in quite straightforward manner. I
therefore pulled myself together and referred him to my father,
about whose consent he did not seem to have any doubts, and he
wished in the first place to have an understanding with myself

there and then. I said 'yes' in the end, while making my parents' ruling a necessary condition. He then spoke formally to the two of them; they showed their satisfaction, agreement was reached subject to the condition, which it was hoped would soon be met, that he should receive further promotion. My sisters and aunts were informed, secrecy being urged upon them most strictly.

Now an admirer had become a fiancé. The difference between the two revealed itself as very considerable. If someone could transform the admirers of all sensible girls into fiancés, it would be a deed of great benefit for our sex, even if this relationship should not be followed by marriage. The love between two people is not diminished in consequence, but becomes more judicious. Countless little follies, all coquetry and moodiness at once disappear. If a fiancé tells us that he likes us better in a morning bonnet than in the most beautiful head-dress, a sensible girl will cease to trouble about her hair-style, and there is nothing more natural than that he too should think in a sound, steady way and should prefer to mould a housewife for himself rather than an ornamental doll for the world at large. And so it goes on in all fields.

If such a girl is at the same time fortunate in that her fiancé possesses understanding and knowledge, she will learn more than high schools and foreign countries can offer. She not only accepts gladly all the education he gives her, but she also tries to bring her own development on further by this path. Love makes possible much that is impossible, and in the end the submission that is so necessary and proper to the female sex will at once catch on; the fiancé does not rule like the married man; he only asks, and his beloved tries to observe what it is he wishes in order to carry out the request even sooner than he asks.

Thus experience has taught me what I would like to have missed for a great deal. I was happy, truly happy, as one can be happy in the world, that is, for a short time.

A summer passed amidst these quiet joys. Narcissus did not give the least reason for complaints; he became even dearer to me, my whole soul hung upon him, he well knew this and knew how to appreciate it. In the meantime out of apparent trivialities there emerged something that gradually became harmful to our relationship.

Narcissus behaved to me as a fiancé and never dared to desire from me that which was forbidden to us. But our opinions differed very much concerning the bounds of virtue and modesty. I wanted to be safe and permitted absolutely no liberty unless it was one that the whole world might know about. He, being used to sweetmeats, found this diet very strict; there was constant contradiction here; he praised my attitude and endeavoured to undermine my resolve.

I thought again of the 'serious' approach of my old language teacher and at the same time of the remedy that I had indicated against it then.

I had become a little more closely acquainted with God again. He had given me so dear a fiancé, and I was grateful to Him for this. Earthly love itself concentrated my spirit and set it in motion, and my concern with God was no contradiction to it. Quite naturally I complained to Him about what was making me anxious and did not notice that I myself wished for and desired what was making me anxious. I saw myself as very strong and did not pray, for instance, 'Lead me not into temptation'; according to my ideas, I had gone far beyond temptation. In this empty show of my own virtue I brazenly appeared before God; He did not repulse me; He left a gentle impression upon my soul after the least movement made towards Him, and this impression moved me to keep on seeking Him again.

The whole world was dead to me apart from Narcissus, nothing apart from him had any attraction for me. Even my love of finery only had the purpose of pleasing him; if I knew that he would not see me, I could not devote any care to it. I liked to dance; but if he was not present, it seemed to me as if I could not bear the movement. For a brilliant festive occasion which he did not attend I could neither procure something new for myself nor adapt something old according to fashion. One person would be as welcome as another, though I might rather say, one would be as burdensome as another. I believed that I had spent the evening really well, if I could arrange a game of cards with some older people, which was something that did not give me the slightest pleasure on other occasions, and if a good elderly friend teased me jokingly about it, I would smile perhaps for the first time the whole evening. It was similar with walks and any social pastimes that can be thought of.

> I had chosen him for myself alone,
> I thought I was born for him on his own,
> His favour was all that I desired.

So I was often solitary while in society, and for the most part I preferred complete solitude. But my restless mind could neither sleep nor dream; I felt and thought, and gradually acquired an aptitude in talking to God about my emotions and thoughts. Then feelings of a different kind developed in my soul which were not

inconsistent with those. For my love of Narcissus was in
accordance with the whole plan of creation and in no way
conflicted with my duties. They were not inconsistent, and yet
they were infinitely different. Narcissus was the only image before
my mind's eye to which my entire love was directed; but the other
feeling did not relate to any image and was inexpressibly pleasant.
I no longer have it and can no longer provide myself with it.

My beloved, who otherwise knew all my secrets, learned
nothing of this. I soon noticed that he thought differently; he
often gave me writings which opposed, with light and heavy
weapons, everything that can be referred to as relationship with
the invisible world. I read the books because they came from him,
and finally did not know a word about anything that was in them.

Discussion of scientific and intellectual matters also did not
take place without disagreement; he behaved like all men, making
fun of women with learning and continually doing things to
educate me. He used to talk to me about all subjects apart from
jurisprudence, and as he constantly brought me writings of all
kinds, he often repeated the questionable doctrine that a woman
must keep her knowledge more secret than a Calvinist his faith in
a Catholic country; and as I really showed myself before the world
in a quite natural way to be no more clever and informed than
was usual, he was the first who was on occasion unable to resist
the vanity of talking about my merits.

A famous man of the world who was much esteemed at that
time on account of his influence, his talents and his mind found
great approval at our court. He treated Narcissus with particular
distinction and had him constantly around him. They also had
arguments about the virtue of women. Narcissus confided
extensively to me their conversation; I was not slow in making my
comments, and my friend asked me for a written essay. I wrote
French fairly fluently: my old master had given me a good
foundation. The correspondence with my friend had been
conducted in this language, and if a more refined form of
education was required, it could only be obtained at that time
from French books. The Count liked my essay; I had to provide a
few little songs which I had written a short time earlier.
Enough—Narcissus seemed to be priding himself on his beloved
without reserve, and the story ended to his great satisfaction with
an ingenious epistle in French verse which the Count sent to him
on the occasion of his departure; it recalled their friendly
controversy and finally congratulated my friend on his good
fortune since after so many doubts and errors he would discover
most surely in the arms of a charming and virtuous wife what
virtue was.

This poem was shown to me before everyone else, but it was then also shown to almost everybody, and everyone could have his own thoughts about it. It happened like this in a number of cases, and in this way all strangers whom he respected had to become known in our house.

A Count's family resided here for a time on account of our skilful doctor. In this house too Narcissus was treated like a son; he introduced me into this circle; agreeable conversation for mind and heart was to be found in the company of these worthy people, and even the usual social pastimes did not seem so empty in this house as elsewhere. Everybody knew that we two were together; we were treated as circumstances might suggest, and our main relationship was left without interference. I mention this one acquaintanceship because it was to have considerable influence upon me in the course of my life.

Now almost a year of our engagement had passed, and with the lapse of this period our springtime had disappeared as well. Summer came, and everything became more serious and warmer.

Through some unexpected deaths posts had become vacant for which Narcissus could be considered as being eligible. The moment was near in which my whole fate was was to be decided, and while Narcissus and all our friends at court took all possible trouble to face certain impressions which were not in his favour, I turned with my concern to the invisible Friend. I was received in such an agreeable manner that I was glad to come again. I confessed quite freely my wish that Narcissus should obtain the post; but my request was not importunate, and I did not demand that it should happen for the sake of my prayers.

The post was given to a much inferior applicant. I was extremely taken aback at the news and hurried into my room, closing the door firmly behind me. My first sorrow resolved itself in tears; my next thought was that this had not after all happened by chance, and at once followed the resolve to accept the situation readily, since even this apparent evil would bring about what was truly best for me. Now the gentlest feelings pressed upon me, dispersing all clouds of trouble; I felt that with this help anything could be borne. I appeared at table in serene mood, to the surprise of others in the house.

Narcissus had less strength than myself, and I had to console him. He had encountered unpleasantness in his own family as well, and with the true trust that existed between us he confided everything to me. His negotiations to enter another state service were also no more successful; I felt it all deeply for his sake and my own, and finally I took everything to that place where my concern was received so well.

The gentler these experiences were, the more frequently I tried to renew them, always seeking consolation at the place where I had so often found it; but I did not always find it: I felt like someone who wishes to get warm in the sunlight and who finds something in the way that casts a shadow. 'What can that be?' I asked myself. I investigated the matter zealously and observed clearly that it all depended on the state of my soul; if it was not wholly turned towards God in the most direct way, I remained cold; I did not feel His reaction and could not hear His response. Now came the second question: 'What is in the way of this turning towards God?' With this I was in a very broad field, and I became involved in an investigation which continued almost through the whole second year of my love story. I could have ended the search earlier, for I soon came upon the track; but I did not want to admit it and looked for a thousand excuses.

I found very soon that the straight direction of my soul was being upset by foolish distractions and preoccupations with unworthy objects; the how and the where were soon clear enough to me. But how should one proceed in a world where everything is indifferent or mad? I would have been glad to let the whole matter be and to go on living in a happy-go-lucky manner like other people too, whom I saw to be in very good spirits; but I was not permitted to: my inner being was too often at variance with myself. If I wanted to withdraw from society and change my circumstances, I could not do so. For now I was restricted within a circle; there were certain bonds that I could not free myself from, and in the matter that was so important to me there was a pressure of frequent misfortunes. I often went to bed in tears and after a sleepless night got up again in the same state; I needed powerful support, and God did not provide this if I ran around in a fool's cap.

Now came a weighing up of each and every activity; dancing and card-playing were the first to be examined. Nothing has ever been said, thought or written for or against these things that I did not look up, discuss, read, consider, augment or reject, and I went to a great deal of trouble. If I gave up these things, I was sure to offend Narcissus; for he was much afraid of that ridiculous approach which the appearance of anxious conscientiousness gives us in the world's eyes. Everything became dreadfully difficult for me because I was now doing things that I considered to be folly, harmful folly, not even because I wanted to, but merely for his sake.

I should not be able to depict without unpleasant prolixity and repetitions the efforts which I made in order to pursue those activities, which in fact distracted and disturbed my inner peace, in such a way that my heart should remain open to the workings of the invisible Being, and how sorrowfully I was compelled to feel that the conflict could not be resolved in this way. For as soon as I put on the dress of folly, it did not remain only a matter of appearance, but folly at once permeated me through and through.

May I be allowed at this point to go beyond the law of a merely historical presentation and to make some observations on what was taking place within me? What could it be that so changed my taste and disposition that in my twenty-second year, indeed earlier, I took no pleasure in things which can provide innocent entertainment to people of this age? I may well answer: just because they were not innocent as far as I was concerned, and because I was not, like others in my position, a stranger to my own soul. No, I knew from experiences which I had obtained without seeking them that there were higher feelings which would truly grant us an enjoyment that we look for in vain from amusements, and that in these higher joys a secret treasure has been stored for our fortification in times of misfortune.

But the sociable pleasures and distractions of youth could not but have a strong fascination for me, because it was not possible for me to take part in them as if I were not participating in them. How much I should now be able to do with great coldness, if I only wanted to, which at that time led me astray, indeed threatened to obtain mastery over me. No middle path was possible here: I had to forego either the delightful entertainments or the refreshing inward emotions.

But the conflict in my soul had already been settled without my being really conscious of it. Even if there was something in me that yearned for sensuous pleasures, I could none the less no longer enjoy them. However fond someone were of wine, he would lose all pleasure in drinking if he found himself with full barrels of wine in a cellar whose putrid air threatened to choke him. Pure air is more than wine, I felt this only too keenly, and from the very start it would have needed little consideration on my part to prefer the good to the alluring, if I had not been prevented by the fear of losing Narcissus's affection. But when finally, after thousandfold conflict and constantly repeated observation, I also cast a sharp eye on the bond that held me to him, I discovered that it was only a weak one and that it could be broken. I discovered all at once that it was only a glass bell that enclosed me in a vacuum; only as much strength again will be needed to break it, and you are saved!

As soon as the thought appeared, the venture was made. I took off the mask and acted on each occasion as I felt in my heart. I was still affectionately fond of Narcissus; but the thermometer that had previously stood in hot water was now suspended in the natural air; it could not rise higher than the warmth of the atmosphere.

Unfortunately the atmosphere became very cold. Narcissus began to withdraw and to behave strangely; he was at liberty to do so; but my thermometer fell as he withdrew. My family noticed it, I was questioned, astonishment was expressed. I declared with manly defiance that I had sacrificed myself already, that I was ready to share all difficulties with him even further, and up to the end of my life; but that I had to demand complete freedom for my actions, and that what I would or would not do had to be dependent upon my convictions; that I would certainly never insist on my own opinion, on the contrary would gladly listen to all arguments, but as this was a matter of my own happiness, the decision had to be mine and I would not tolerate any kind of compulsion. Just as the reasoning of the greatest doctor would not persuade me to accept a food that was perhaps otherwise completely nutritious and much liked by many people, as soon as my own experience proved to me that this food was harmful to me at all times (as, for instance, I might quote the use of coffee), so and indeed even more emphatically would I refuse to consider that any action which caused me confusion could be morally acceptable to me.

As I had been preparing myself so long on the quiet, the discussions about this topic were for me pleasant rather than disagreeable. I allowed my heart its freedom and felt the full value of my decision. I did not yield an inch, and anyone to whom I did not owe childlike respect received rough treatment. At home I was soon victorious. From her youth onwards my mother had similar views, only in her case they had not come to maturity; no trouble had pressed upon her and strengthened her courage to implement her conviction. She was happy to see her unspoken wishes fulfilled through myself. My younger sister seemed to be following me; the second sister was observant and quiet. It was my aunt who made most objections. The reasons which she brought forward seemed irrefutable to her, and indeed were so, because they were wholly general. In the end I was compelled to show her that she in no way had a voice in the matter, and it was only rarely that she revealed that she was persisting in her viewpoint. She was also the only person who observed this business from close to and remained wholly unemotional. I am not doing her an injustice when I say that she had no feeling and the most limited ideas.

Father behaved completely in accordance with his way of thinking. He did not talk a great deal with me about the matter, but he did so fairly frequently, and his reasons were sensible, and, as *his* reasons, irrefutable; and the deep conviction of my being in the right gave me the strength to argue with him. But soon the scene changed; I had to appeal to his feelings. Compelled by his reasoning, I broke into highly emotional expostulations. I gave free rein to my tongue and my tears. I showed him how much I loved Narcissus and what constrictions I had been posing on myself in the last two years, how sure I was that I was acting rightly, that I was ready to put my seal upon this certainty with the loss of the beloved fiancé and of apparent happiness, indeed, if it were necessary, with all my goods and chattels; that I would rather leave my country, parents and friends and earn my bread in a foreign land than act against my convictions. He concealed his feeling, kept silent for some time and finally declared himself in public in my favour.

From then onwards Narcissus avoided coming to our house, and then my father gave up the weekly social gathering which he visited. The affair caused a stir at court and in the city. People talked about it as they usually do in such cases where the public is in the habit of taking intense interest, because it is spoilt, in being able to have some influence on the decisions of weak spirits. I was sufficiently acquainted with the world, and knew that one is often blamed for something by the very people whom one has allowed to persuade oneself to that course of action, and, even without this, in the state of the inner self all such transient opinions would have meant less than nothing to me.

On the other hand I did not deny myself indulgence in my fondness for Narcissus. I could no longer see him, and my heart had not changed towards him. I loved him dearly, as it were anew and in a steadier way than before. If he could agree not to disturb my convictions, I would be his; without this condition I would have refused to share a kingdom with him. For several months I took these feelings and thoughts around with me, and as I at last felt calm and strong enough to set about things in a quiet and sedate way, I wrote him a polite note, not a tender one, and asked him why he was no longer coming to see me.

As I knew his way of being reluctant to explain himself, even in minor matters, but of getting on quietly with what he thought best, I deliberately wrote in pressing terms. I received a long and, as it seemed to me, insipid reply written in a rambling style and with insignificant clichés, to the effect that he could not settle down and offer me his hand without a better position, that nobody knew better than I what obstacles he had encountered up to now, that he believed a long, continued and fruitless association could harm my reputation, and that I should permit him to keep himself at the same distance as up to now; as soon as he was in a position to make me happy, his word that he had given me would be sacred.

I answered him immediately, saying that as the affair was known to everybody it would be too late to salvage my reputation, and for this my conscience and my innocence were the best sureties; but that I herewith released him from his promise without hesitation and wished that he would thereby be helped to find his happiness. Within the hour I received a short answer which was in essentials completely identical with the first. He insisted that on receipt of an appointment he would ask me if I would be willing to share his happiness with him.

As far as I was concerned, that was as good as saying nothing at all. I told my friends and relations that the business had been settled, and indeed it was too. For when nine months later he was promoted in a very desirable way, he offered me his hand once more, to be sure, with the proviso that I would have to change my views as wife of a man who had to live in a certain style. I refused politely and hastened in heart and mind away from this episode, just as one longs to be away from the theatre once the curtain has fallen. And as shortly afterwards he made a rich and reputable match, as it was now very easy for him to do, and as I knew that he was happy after his fashion, my ease of mind was complete.

I may not pass over in silence the fact that a number of impressive proposals of marriage were made to me, some even before he received his appointment, some also afterwards; however, I rejected them without any hesitation, although Father and Mother would have wished for more tractability on my part.

Now it seemed as if after a stormy March and April the most beautiful May weather was being bestowed upon me. I enjoyed an indescribable peace of mind at the same time as good health; however much I looked in the world around me, for all my loss I had still won. Young and full of feeling as I was, creation seemed to me a thousand times more beautiful than before, when I had to have society and games so that time did not become too heavy for me in the beautiful garden. As I was not ashamed of my piety, I had the courage not to conceal my love of arts and sciences. I sketched, painted, read and found enough people who gave me support; instead of the great world that I had left, or rather which left me, a smaller one formed itself around me, one that was far richer and more entertaining. I had a liking for social life, and I do not deny that I dreaded loneliness when I gave up my previous acquaintances. Now I found that I was sufficiently, indeed perhaps too much, recompensed. My contacts now really did become extended, not only with local people whose views coincided with mine, but also with strangers. My story had got about, and many people were curious to see the girl who esteemed God more than her fiancé. In any case, at that time a certain religious atmosphere was noticeable in Germany. In several houses of princes and counts there was active care for the salvation of the soul. There was no lack of aristocratic families who cherished the same watchfulness, and among the lower classes this attitude was very widespread.

The count's family that I mentioned above now drew me closer to themselves. In the meantime they had been reinforced by the advent of some relations in the city. These estimable people sought my company, as I did theirs. They had extended connections, and in this house I became acquainted with a great number of the princes, counts and gentlemen of the Empire. My opinions were a secret to no one, and whether people respected them or only treated them with consideration, I accomplished my purpose and was spared vexation.

In yet another way I was to be led back into the world. At that time a stepbrother of my father's, who had only visited us in passing on other occasions, stayed with us for a fairly long period. He had given up the service of his court, where he had been respected and had had influence, solely because everything had not gone as he thought it should. His intellect was accurate and his character strict, and in this he was very similar to my father; only the latter had at the same time a certain degree of pliability which made it easier for him to give way in business matters and not to do something against his convictions, but to let it happen and then to give vent to his anger about it either quietly to himself or in confidence with his family. My uncle was much younger, and his independence was supported not a little by his outer circumstances. He had had a very rich mother and had hopes of another great fortune from her near and distant relatives; he was in no need of an extra allowance from outside, whereas my father was firmly attached by his salary to court service, since his own private means were moderate.

My uncle had become even more unbending as a result of domestic misfortune. He had lost at an early stage a dear wife and a promising son, and from that time onwards he seemed to wish to remove from his path everything that was not dependent upon his will.

In the family it was occasionally whispered with a certain complacency that he would probably not marry again and that we children could already regard ourselves as heirs of his great fortune. I paid no further attention to this; but the behaviour of the others was affected not a little by these hopes. With his tenacity of character he had got into the habit of contradicting nobody in discussion, and rather of listening in a friendly manner to everyone's opinion and to emphasizing further himself the way each person thought of a matter by means of arguments and examples. Someone who did not know him always believed that he was in agreement with him; for he had a dominating intellect and could put himself imaginatively into all types of mind. It did not work out so well for him as far as I was concerned, for here there was talk of feelings concerning which he had no idea at all, and however considerately, sympathetically and understandingly he spoke to me about my views, it was none the less remarkable to me that he obviously had no conception of what lay at the basis of all my actions.

Secretive as he was moreover, the purpose of his unusual stay with us did become clear after some time. As could eventually be observed, he had picked out from among us our youngest sister in order to marry her and make her happy according to his lights; and indeed, with her physical and intellectual gifts, especially if a considerable fortune was also to be taken into account, she could lay claim to the very best offers of marriage. He revealed his views about myself, as it were in pantomimic manner, by procuring for me a place as a canoness; I was very soon drawing the income from this.[1]

My sister was not so pleased with his solicitude nor so grateful for it as I was. She revealed to me an affair of the heart which she had hitherto very wisely concealed: for she was afraid of what in fact really happened, that I would advise her in every possible way against the association with a man who should not have found her favour. I did my uttermost, and was successful. The Uncle's intentions were too serious and explicit and the prospect for my sister, with her outlook, too attractive for her not to feel bound to have the strength to give up an inclination which her reason itself disapproved of.

As she no longer avoided the Uncle's gentle guidance, as she had done before, the foundation to his plan was soon laid. She

---

1. There were religious establishments for aristocratic ladies in Germany at this time which allowed their members to make use of income and to live where they pleased. (Tr.)

became a lady in waiting at a nearby court where he could give her in charge of a friend, who was highly regarded as a court superintendent, for purposes of supervision and education. I accompanied her to the place of her new abode. We could both be very pleased with the reception which we were given, and I often had to smile secretly about the role which I now played in the world as a canoness, as a young and pious canoness.

In earlier times such a relationship would have confused me very much, indeed would perhaps have turned my head; but now I was very composed, for all that surrounded me. I allowed my hair to be attended to for some hours in great tranquility, decked myself out and thought nothing of it, except that in my circumstances I was in duty bound to put on this gala livery. In the crowded rooms I talked to all and sundry without any figure or character making a strong impression on me. When I returned home, tired legs were usually the only sensation I brought back with me. The many people whom I saw were useful to my understanding; and I learnt to appreciate some women, in particular the court superintendent under whose guidance my sister had the good fortune of being educated, as models of all human virtues and of good and noble behaviour.

Yet on my return I did not feel such felicitous physical consequences from this journey. In spite of great abstemiousness and careful dieting I was not, as I usually was, master of my own time and energies. Sustenance, movement, getting up and going to bed, getting dressed and going out were not dependent on my own will and feeling, as they were at home. In the round of social events one may not stand still without being impolite, and I was glad to carry out everything that was necessary because I took it to be my duty, because I knew that it would soon be over, and because I felt fitter than I had ever done. In spite of these things, this strange restless life must have affected me more strongly than I realized. For I had scarcely reached home and delighted my parents with a satisfying narrative than I was overcome by a haemorrhage which, although it was not dangerous and passed quickly, all the same left me for a long time with a noticeable weakness.

This proved to be another lesson I had to learn. I was glad to do so. Nothing bound me to the world, and I was convinced that I would never find the right path here, and therefore I was in a most serene and calm state, and while I had given up all claim to life, I was kept alive.

I had to bear with a new affliction, as my mother was overcome by an oppressive malady which she suffered a further five years before she paid her debt to nature. During this time there was much to exercise us. Often when her fears grew too strong, she had us all summoned to her bedside in the night, so that she might at least be distracted, if not made better, by our presence. The pressure when my father also began to be ailing was heavier, indeed scarcely bearable. From his youth onwards he frequently had severe headaches, though these lasted at most only thirty-six hours. But now they became continuous and when they reached a certain high degree of intensity, the misery of it broke my heart. It was during these storms that I was mostly aware of my physical weakness, because it prevented me from carrying out my most sacred and my dearest duties, or anyhow, it made their practice extremely difficult.

Now I could examine myself to see whether the road which I had taken was truth or fantasy, whether perhaps I had only followed others in their thought, or whether the object of my belief had reality, and to my very great comfort and support I always found the latter to be the case. I had sought and found the straight direction of my heart to God, and the company of the 'beloved ones', and this was what made everything easier for me. Just as the traveller makes for the shade, so my soul hastened to this place of refuge when everything was pressing upon me from outside, and never came back empty.

In recent times some protagonists of religion, who seem to have more zeal for it than sensitivity, have invited their fellow-believers to publicize examples of real answers to prayer, presumably because they wanted to have a sure pledge in order to attack their opponents in a really diplomatic and juridical way. How little must true feeling be known to them, and how few genuine experiences can they have had themselves!

I may say that I never came back empty-handed after I had sought God when under pressure and in distress. This is saying a great deal, but I cannot and may not say more. Although every experience was very important for me in the critical moment, the story of it would be dull, insignificant and improbable, if I were to quote individual instances. How happy I was that a thousand little events together proved to me, as surely as drawing breath is a sign of life, that I was not without God in the world. He was close to me, I stood before Him. That is what I can say most truthfully, with a deliberate avoidance of all formal theological language.

How I wished that in those days too I had been without formal doctrine; but who comes at an early stage to the good fortune of being aware of his own self, without alien forms and in pure coherence? I was in earnest about my salvation. Modestly I trusted

to the reputation of strangers: I gave myself up completely to the
Halle conversion system,[1] and my whole personality could in no
way fit into it.

According to this teaching the change of heart had to begin
with a deep dread of sin; in this distress the heart has to be aware,
sometimes to a greater and sometimes to a lesser degree, of the
punishment that is deserved, and to have a foretaste of hell which
embitters the pleasures of sin. Finally there has to be an
awareness of a very perceptible assurance of grace, though this is
often lost sight of as time goes on and has to be earnestly searched
for again.

Nothing of all this applied in my case, neither closely nor
remotely. When I honestly sought God, He let Himself be found
and did not reproach me about things from the past. Certainly I
saw afterwards where I had been unworthy and knew also where I
still was unworthy; but the awareness of my failings was devoid of
all fear. Not for a moment did I have any fear of hell, indeed the
idea of an evil spirit and of a place of punishment and torture
after death could in no way find a place in the circle of my ideas. I
found that the people who lived without God and whose hearts
were closed to faith in and love for the Invisible One were already
so unhappy that, as I saw it, a hell and physical punishments
seemed rather to promise an alleviation of the punishment than
an intensification of it. I could only see people in this world who
allowed room in their hearts for malicious feelings, who were
obdurate against the good in any shape or form and urged evil
upon themselves and others, and who preferred to shut their eyes
by day, simply in order to be able to assert that the sun gave no
light—how inexpressively wretched these people seemed to me!
Who could have created a hell to worsen their condition!

This attitude of mind remained with me, on one day as much as
on another, for ten years. It was maintained through many trials,
even on the painful deathbed of my dear mother. I was frank
enough not to conceal my cheerful disposition on this occasion
from pious, but systematically and wholly orthodox people, and I
had to put up with many a friendly reprimand about it. They
believed they were laying before me just at the right time how
much earnestness was required in order to lay a good foundation
in days of health.

I also did not want there to be a lack of earnestness. I allowed
myself to be convinced for the moment, and for the life of me

1. Halle was the main centre of the pietistic religious movement founded
by August Hermann Francke (1663-1727). (Tr.)

would have loved to be sad and full of terror. But how astonished I was that, once and for all, it was not possible for me. When I thought of God I was cheerful and pleased; even during my dear mother's painful end I had no dread of death. But in those great hours I learnt much, and quite different things than my officious instructors believed.

Gradually I became dubious about the insights of many very famous people, and kept my opinions to myself. A certain friend, a lady to whom I had conceded too much at first, constantly wanted to interfere in my affairs; I was compelled to dissociate myself from her too, and on one occasion I told her quite definitely that she should not take trouble, I did not need her advice; that I knew my God and wished to have Him wholly alone as my guide. She was very offended, and I believe she has never completely forgiven me.

This decision to withdraw from the advice and influence of my friends in religious matters had as result that I gained the courage to go my own way in outward concerns as well. Things could have gone badly with me without the support of my faithful invisible Guide, and even now I have to express my astonishment at this wise and happy leading. Nobody really knew what it was that was affecting me, and I did not know myself.

That thing, the hitherto unexplained evil thing, which separates us from the Being to Whom we owe our life, from the Being from Whom everything that can be called life draws its sustenance, that thing which is called sin was as yet not known to me at all.

In the fellowship of the invisible Friend I experienced the sweetest enjoyment of all my life's energies. The desire to enjoy this happiness always was so great that I was glad to desist from anything that would disturb this association, and in this respect experience was my best teacher. However, what happened to me was comparable to what happens to sick people who have no medicine and attempt to help themselves by a diet. It does something, but by no means enough.

I could not always remain in solitude, although I found it to be the best means against the distraction of thoughts so peculiar to myself. Whenever I came back into the crowd afterwards, it made all the more impression on me. My most particular advantage was my predominant love of stillness, and in the end I always withdrew again to the quiet. As if in a kind of half-light, I recognized my own wretchedness and weakness, and I endeavoured to help myself by sparing myself and not exposing myself.

I had exercised my dietetic care for seven years long. I did not consider myself to be bad and found my condition desirable. Unless there had been special circumstances and conditions I should have remained at this level, and I only came further by means of a strange path. Against the advice of all my friends I started a new relationship. Their objections surprised me at first. I at once turned to my invisible Guide and as He did not begrudge me the relationship, I continued without misgivings on my way.

A man of intellect, heart and talents had acquired property in the neighbourhood. He and his family were among the strangers whom I got to know as well. We found ourselves in agreement in our manners, habits and approach to household matters, and could therefore soon become linked with one another.

Philo—I will call him by this name—was no longer a young man and he could be of great assistance in certain business affairs to my father, whose strength was beginning to decline. He soon became an intimate friend of the house, and we quickly became close friends since, as he put it, he found in me a person who was without both the extravagant and empty qualities of the world of society and also the dry and anxious features of the pietists. I liked him very much, and he was very useful to me.

Although I did not have any gift or inclination for intervening in worldly affairs and seeking to have any influence, I liked to hear about things and to know what was going on, both near at hand and at a distance. With regard to worldly matters I liked to obtain for myself an unfeeling clarity of perception; I preserved the qualities of feeling, inwardness and inclination for my God, my family and my friends.

These latter were, if I may say so, jealous of my association with Philo, and yet they were right from more than one point of view to warn me. I suffered a great deal on the quiet, for I could not myself consider their objections to be wholly empty or self-centred. From earliest days I had been accustomed to subordinating my own views, but this time my convictions would not submit. I implored my God to warn, prevent or guide me in this matter too, and as after these prayers my heart did not dissuade me, I continued on my path with great courage.

In a general way Philo bore a slight similarity to Narcissus; only a pious education had held together and invigorated his emotional life more emphatically. He had less vanity and more character, and if the former was subtle, exact, persistent and untiring in worldly business matters, the latter was clear, sharp and quick, and someone who worked with incredible facility. Through him I learnt about the intimate circumstances of almost all the distinguished people whose outward appearances I had got to know in society, and I was pleased to watch the turmoil from my distant vantage-point. Philo could no longer hide anything from me: he gradually confided to me his outward and his inward connections. I was afraid for him, for I could anticipate certain circumstances and complications, and the evil came more quickly than I had assumed; for he had always been reticent with certain confessions, and even in the end he only revealed to me so much that I could conjecture the worst.

How this affected my heart! I came to experiences which were quite new to me. With indescribable sadness I saw an Agathon[1] who had been brought up in the groves of Delphi, who still owed his apprentice's premium and was now repaying it with heavy arrears of interest, and this Agathon was my closely linked friend. My sympathy was impassioned and complete; I suffered and we both found ourselves in a very unusual position.

After I had spent a lot of time considering his state of mind, my observations turned to myself. The thought that you are not better than he is rose before me like a small cloud, spread gradually and darkened my whole soul.

Now I was not merely thinking that I was not better than he; I could feel it, and I felt it in such a way that I would not care to feel it again: and it was no quick transition. For more than a year I was compelled to have the feeling that if an invisible hand had not been supporting me, I could have become a Girard, a Cartouche, a Damiens[2], or whatever monster one may care to mention: I sensed the potentiality in my heart; God, what a discovery!

If up to now I had not been able even to the slightest degree to be aware through experience of the reality of sin in myself, the possibility of sin had become most terribly clear to me in the form of premonition, and yet I did not know the evil, I was only afraid of it, I felt that I could be guilty, and had no cause to accuse myself.

Deeply convinced as I was that such a type of mind as I had to acknowledge mine to be could not be appropriate for a unification with the highest Being after death, as I wished, I had little fear of

1. Agathon is the hero of Wieland's novel *Geschichte des Agathon* (1766-67). (Tr.)

2. Jean Baptiste Girard (1680-1733) was wrongly believed to be the seducer of a child. Louis-Dominique Cartouche (1693-1721) was leader of a robber-band. Robert-François Damiens (1714-1757) attempted to assassinate Louis XV of France. (Tr.)

coming to such a state of separation. In spite of all the evil that I discovered in myself, I loved Him and hated what I felt, indeed I wanted to hate it even more seriously, and my whole desire was to be released from this illness and from this disposition to illness, and I was sure that the great Doctor would not refuse me his help.

The only question was: what would make good this damage? Exercises in virtue? I could not even think of these; for I had been practising for ten years something that was already more than mere virtue, and the horrors that had now been recognized had meanwhile lain hidden in my soul. Could they not have also broken loose as in the case of David when he caught sight of Bathsheba, and was he not also a friend of God, and was I not convinced deeply within myself that God was my Friend?

Was it to be, therefore, perhaps an unavoidable weakness of humanity? Must we then be resigned to the prospect of feeling the dominating power of our inclinations at some time or other, and with the best will in the world is there nothing we can do apart from abhorring the fall that we have had and falling again when similar circumstances arise?

I could derive no consolation from moral philosophy. I could be satisfied neither by its severity, with which it tries to overcome our inclinations, nor by its complaisance, with which it would like to make our inclinations into virtues. The basic ideas which association with the invisible Friend had brought me already had a much more decisive value for me.

When I studied the songs which David had written after that ugly catastrophe, I was very much struck by the fact that he saw the evil within himself as being already present in the substance from which he had been made, but that he wanted to be absolved from his sins and that he prayed most ardently for a pure heart.

But by what means was he now to attain this? Of course I knew the answer from the symbolic books: it was known to me as a Biblical truth that the blood of Jesus Christ would purify us from all sins. It was only now, however, that I noticed that I had never as yet understood this so frequently repeated saying. The questions: 'What does that mean? How is it intended to happen?' were at work within me day and night. Finally I believed that I could see dimly, as if in a half-light, that what I was seeking was to be sought in the incarnation of the eternal Word through which all things and we ourselves too have been created. It was revealed to me, as if in a twilight distance, that the primal Being once came to dwell in the depths where we are caught and which He sees through and embraces, that He went step by step through our condition, from conception and birth to the grave, and that He has risen, by means of this strange détour, once more to the bright high places where we too should be living in order to be happy.

Oh why must we, in order to talk of such things, use images which only point to outward circumstances? Where before Him is there anything that is high or deep, dark or bright? It is only we who have a below and above, a day and a night. And for that very reason did He become like us, because otherwise we would not be able to have any part of Him.

But how can we participate in this inestimable blessing? Through faith, the scriptures answer us. And what is faith? How can accepting the account of an occurrence as true be of help to me? I must be able to claim its effects and consequences as my own. This appropriating faith must be a peculiar state of mind, one that is not usual to natural man.

'Now, Almighty One, grant me faith!' I once implored when under the greatest emotional pressure. I leaned over a little table at which I was sitting and hid my tear-stained face in my hands. At this point I was in the position that we have to be in, if God is to pay heed to our prayers, and one in which we seldom are.

Indeed, if only anyone could portray what I felt then! A pressure drew my soul towards the cross on which Jesus once turned pale; it was a pressure, I cannot call it anything else, fully resembling that pressure which draws our soul to an absent lover, an approach that is presumably much more fundamental and truthful than we assume. In this way my soul drew near to Him Who had become a man and Who had died on the cross, and in that moment I knew what fate was.

'That is faith!' I said and leaped up, as if half-terrified. I tried now to be sure of my feeling and my intuition, and in a short time I had become convinced that my spirit had received a capacity to soar upwards that was quite new to it.

Words fail us in the light of these experiences. I could distinguish them quite clearly from any imaginings; they were wholly without the element of imagination and without images. and yet they provided as much certainty of reference to an object as does the imagination when it paints for us the features of an absent beloved.

When the first rapture was over I noticed that I had already been familiar with this condition of the soul at an earlier time; but I had never felt it in this strength. I had never been able to hold it fast nor keep it as my own. I believe generally that every human soul has felt something of this at one time or another. Without doubt it is *this* that teaches everyone that there is a God.

Up to now I had been very content with this strength, which

had only previously come upon me from time to time, and if the unexpected trouble had not befallen me for the last year or so through a strange dispensation of Providence, and if in consequence my strength and ability in my own eyes had not lost all credit, I should perhaps have remained content with that condition.

But now I had acquired wings since that great moment. I could rise above what had been threatening me earlier, as without effort a bird flies singing over the fast river, before which a little dog halts, anxiously barking.

My joy was indescribable, and although I dislosed nothing about it to anyone, those around me did notice an unusual cheerfulness on my part, without being able to understand what the cause of my pleasure might be. If only I had kept silent and endeavoured to preserve the pure disposition in my soul! If only I had not let myself be led astray by circumstances, so that I came forward with my secret! Then I would have been able once again to save myself a long détour.

Since in my previous ten years' course as a Christian this necessary strength had not been in my soul, I had found myself also in the position of other honest people; I had helped myself by always filling my imagination with images relating to God, and this too is already genuinely useful: for it staves off harmful pictures and their evil consequences. Then our soul often seizes hold of one or another of the mental images and soars upward a little with them, as a young bird flutters from one branch to another. As long as one does not have anything better, this exercise is indeed not to be rejected completely.

Images and impressions aiming at God are provided for us by church institutions, bells, organs, singing and especially the discourses of our teachers. I was quite inexpressibly eager for them: neither inclement weather nor physical weakness prevented me from visiting the churches, and only the sounding of Sunday bells could cause me a certain impatience on my bed of sickness. I very much liked to hear our court superintendent chaplain, who was an excellent man; I esteemed his colleagues too, and I was able to pick out the golden apples of the divine word even from earthly vessels amid ordinary fruit. All kinds of private acts of edification, as they are called, were added to the public exercises, and in this way too the imagination and a refined sensuousness were encouraged. I was so used to this way, I respected it so much that even now nothing higher came to my mind. For my soul only has feelers and not eyes; it only gropes its way and does not see; oh, that it could receive eyes and be allowed to see!

Even now I went full of desire to hear the sermons; but alas, what was happening to me? I no longer found what I had found previously. These preachers were blunting their teeth on the shells while I enjoyed the kernel. Now I could not but become tired of them soon; but I was too spoilt to content myself alone with Him Whom I knew how to find already. I wanted to have pictures, I needed outward impressions, and I believed that I was experiencing a pure, spiritual requirement.

Philo had been in association with the Moravian Church[1]; his library still contained many writings by the Count. On several occasions he had talked to me in very clear and fair terms about the matter and had requested me to look through some of these writings, even if it were only to become acquainted with a psychological phenomenon. I thought that the Count was really too awful a heretic; so I also left the Ebersdorf hymnbook alone which my friend had, as it were, pressed upon me with similar intention.

With a complete lack of all outer means to enlivenment, I turned as if by chance to this particular hymnbook, and to my astonishment really found hymns in it which, admittedly in very strange forms, seemed to be interpreting what I felt; the originality and naivety of the expressions attracted me. Personal emotions seemed to be expressed in a particular way; there was no school terminology to recall something stiff or commonplace. I was convinced that these people felt what I felt, and I was very happy to commit to memory a characteristic verse and to sustain myself with it for some days.

From the particular moment in which the truth had been given to me about three months had passed in this way. At last I made up my mind to reveal everything to my friend Philo and to ask him to let me have those writings about which I had now become exceptionally curious. I really did this too, in spite of the fact that something in my heart advised me strongly against it.

I told Philo the whole story in detail, and as he himself was one of the chief characters in it, since my narrative contained a

1. The Moravian Church originated in the fifteenth century in the east of the present Czechoslovakia. At the outbreak of the Thirty Years War this branch of Protestantism suffered a severe defeat which greatly reduced its activities. Count von Zinzendorf (1700–60) invited a colony of the Moravian Brethren to settle on his estate in Saxony, when they were subject to persecution in Bohemia, and to build the town of Herrnhut. A copy of the Ebersdorf hymnbook (1742) was to be found in the Goethe family house. (Tr.)

particularly severe penitential sermon for him as well, he was
most taken aback and moved. He dissolved into tears. I was
pleased, and believed that in his case too a complete change of
attitude had been effected.

He provided me with all the writings I could ask for, and now I
had superfluous food for my imagination. I made great progress in
the Zinzendorf way of thinking and talking. It should not be
thought that I do not know how to value the Count's approach at
present too; I am glad for justice to be done to him; he is no empty
dreamer; he speaks of great truths mostly in bold flights of the
imagination, and those who have scorned him were incapable of
either esteeming or distinguishing his qualities.

I became prodigiously fond of him. If I had been my own
master, I would certainly have left my country and friends, and
would have joined him; inevitably we should have understood one
another, and we should not have got on together for long without
difficulty.

Thanks be to my guardian spirit which kept me at that time so
limited in my household situation! It was already a big journey for
me if I only went into the garden of the house. Caring for my old
and ailing father gave me work enough, and in leisure hours noble
imagination was my pastime. The only person whom I saw was
Philo, whom my father loved greatly, but whose open relationship
to myself had somewhat suffered as a result of the last avowal. In
his case the feeling had not penetrated deeply, and as some
attempts by him to talk in my language had not been successful,
he found it all the easier to avoid this subject-matter as he was
able, with his extended knowledge, to keep on introducing new
topics of conversation.

So I was a Moravian sister on my own responsibility, and was
constrained to conceal this new turning of my feelings and
inclinations in particular from the superintendent chaplain, whom
I had good cause to esteem as my father-confessor and whose
great merits were not diminished in my eyes even now by his
extreme dislike of the Moravian community. Unfortunately this
worthy man was to experience much distress because of myself
and others!

A number of years ago he had got to know elsewhere a
gentleman and to recognize him as an honest, pious man, and he
had kept up an uninterrupted correspondence with him as
someone who was earnestly seeking God. How distressing it
was for his spiritual guide, therefore, when this gentleman
subsequently had dealings with the Moravian community and
stayed for a long period among the Brethren; how agreeable it was

on the other hand when his friend fell out again with the Brethren, made up his mind to live near him and appeared to be submitting completely to his leadership once more.

Now the new arrival was presented, as it were in triumph, to all the particularly loved lambs in the superintendent shepherd's flock. It was only into our house that he was not introduced, because my father was not in the habit of seeing anyone any more. The gentleman received great approbation; he possesed the well-bred manner of the court and the engaging style of the Moravians, as well as many fine natural attributes, and soon became the great saint for everybody with whom he became acquainted, which was particularly pleasing to his clerical patron. Unfortunately the gentleman had only quarrelled with the Moravian community about outward manners and in his heart was still wholly theirs. It is true, he really held to the reality of the matter; only he too found the frippery that the Count had hung around it highly acceptable. He was after all accustomed to those ways of presentation and talking, and if he now had to hide himself carefully from his old friend, he found it all the more necessary to come with his little verses, litanies and pictures as soon as he saw a small group of close acquaintances and, as can be imagined, he found great applause.

I did not know anything about the whole business and went on with frippery in my own way. We did not meet for a long time.

Once, in a free hour, I visited a sick friend. I met several acquaintances at this lady's and soon noticed that I had disturbed them in a discussion. I acted as if I had noticed nothing, but to my great surprise saw on the wall some Moravian pictures, in graceful frames. I quickly grasped what might have happened during the time when I had not been in the house, and welcomed this new phenomenon with some suitable verses.

You can imagine my women friends' astonishment. We declared where we stood and were united and on terms of intimacy at once.

Now I often looked for an opportunity to go out. Unfortunately I only found one every three or four weeks, but became acquainted with the aristocratic apostle and gradually with the whole secret community. When I could, I visited their meetings, and with my sociable temperament it was extremely pleasant for me to hear from others and to pass on to others what I had hitherto worked out only in and with myself.

I was not so captivated that I did not notice how only a few sensed the meaning of the delicate words and phrases and how they had not been more benefited by them than previously by the symbolic church language. In spite of this I continued with them and did not let myself be confused. It seemed to me that I had not been called to make investigations and examine hearts. After all I too had been prepared for something better by means of many an innocent exercise. I regarded my contribution as of little importance, and when I did speak I insisted on seeking the meaning which in the case of such delicate topics is covered up rather than intimated by words; otherwise I let everybody go their own way with an attitude of quiet conciliation.

These restful times of secret social pleasure were soon followed by the storms of public controversies and unpleasantness which caused a great stir at court and in the city and, I might almost say, provoked many a scandal. The time had come when our court superintendent chaplain, that great opponent of the Moravian community, was to learn to his blessed mortification that the best and otherwise most attached members of his congregation all favoured the community. He was extremely hurt, in the first moment forgot all moderation and was subsequently unable to withdraw, even if he had wanted to. There were vehement debates during which I was fortunately not named, since I was only a chance member of the meetings that were so much hated and our zealous leader could not do without my father and my friend in lay matters. I kept to my neutrality with quiet contentment, for it was upsetting for me to talk about such emotions and topics even with people of good will, if they could not grasp the deepest level of meaning and only lingered on the surface. But now indeed it did seem useless, in fact harmful, to be quarrelling with adversaries about a subject concerning which it was difficult to find agreement among friends. For I could soon notice that kind and noble-spirited people who in this instance could not keep their hearts free from resentment and hate very soon passed on to injustice and, in order to defend an outward form, almost destroyed their best, inward self.

However much the worthy man may have been wrong in this case and for all the attempts that were made to arouse me against him, I could never withhold my heartfelt respect from him. I knew him precisely; I could in fairness put myself into his way of looking at these things. I had never met a human being without weaknesses; but these are more noticeable in the case of outstanding people. Once and for all, we wish and desire that those who are so very privileged should also not pay any tribute or dues. I respected him as an excellent man and hoped to use the influence of my quiet neutrality if not to obtain peace, then perhaps an armistice. I do not know what I would have effected; God interpreted the matter more briefly and took him to Himself.

At his bier all those who had been quarrelling with him about words shortly beforehand were in tears. No one had ever doubted his integrity and his fear of God.

At this time I too had to put aside the playthings which to a certain extent had appeared in another light because of these controversies. The Uncle had quietly carried through his plans with respect to my sister. He introduced a young man of rank and wealth to her as her fiancé and provided a generous dowry, as could be expected from him. My father gladly consented; my sister was fancy-free and had been prepared, and was glad to change her station. The wedding was to take place at the Uncle's castle, family and friends had been invited, and we all came in a cheerful spirit.

For the first time in my life entry into a house aroused admiration in me. I had often heard tell of the Uncle's good taste, of his Italian architect, his collections and his library; but I compared all that with what I had already seen and made a very variegated picture out of it in my thoughts. How surprised I was therefore at the serious and harmonious impression that I received on entering the house and which became strengthened in every hall and room. If elsewhere pomp and embellishment had only been a distraction as far as I was concerned, here I felt composed and led back to myself. What is more, splendour and dignity in all the arrangements for the solemnities and festivities evoked quiet pleasure, and it was just as incomprehensible to me that one man could have invented and arranged all this as that a number of people could have co-operated in order to be effective together with such great significance. And in the midst of all this the host and those around him seemed so natural; no traces of stiffness nor of empty ceremonial were to be perceived.

The wedding ceremony itself was introduced unexpectedly and in a heartfelt manner; excellent vocal music took us by surprise, and the clergyman knew how to give this ceremony all the solemnity of truth. I was standing by Philo, and instead of congratulating me he said with a deep sigh: 'When I saw your sister offer her hand, I felt as if I had had boiling-hot water poured over me.' 'Why?' I asked. 'This always happens to me when I witness a marriage ceremony,' he replied. I laughed at him, and since then I have had occasion to think of his words frequently enough.

The cheerfulness of the company, which included many young people, seemed twice as sparkling since everything surrounding us was dignified and serious. All household furniture, table-linen, table-services and centre-pieces blended with the whole, and if in

other contexts the architects appeared to have come from one
school together with the confectioners, here confectioner and
table-planner had been pupils of the architect.

As the company was remaining together for several days, the
gifted and intelligent host had made very varied arrangements for
their entertainment. I did not repeat here the sad experience
which I had had so often in my life of finding what a bad position
a large, mixed gathering is in when, left to itself, it has to have
recourse to the most general and shallow ways of spending the
time, with the result that it is the good rather than the bad folk
that feel the lack of entertainment.

The Uncle had arranged things quite differently. He had
appointed two or three marshals, if I may refer to them thus; the
one had to look after the entertainment of the young people:
dances, drives by carriage and little games were devised and
organized by him, and as young people are glad to be out-of-doors
and do not shrink from the influences of fresh air, they were given
the use of the garden and of the assembly room overlooking the
garden; some galleries and pavilions had been built on to the
assembly room for this special purpose, and although they were
only constructed of boards and canvas, their proportions were so
noble that they gave the impression of being exclusively stone and
marble.

How rarely a festivity takes place where he who calls together
the guests also feels an obligation to care for their needs and
comfort in every way!

Hunting, games of cards, short walks and opportunities for
confidential conversations of an individual nature had been
prepared for the older people, and he who went soonest to bed was
also certain to have been given a room that was farthest from any
noise.

Because of this good organization the space where we found
ourselves appeared to be a little world, and yet when looked at
more closely the castle was not large, and it would no doubt have
been difficult to have accommodated so many people there and to
have shown appropriate hospitality to everyone without precise
knowledge of the premises and without the ingeniousness of the
host.

Just as the sight of a well-proportioned person is pleasing to us,
so too is a whole piece of arrangement out of which the presence
of an intelligent, sensible character can be perceived. It is in itself
pleasurable to come into a tidy house, even if in other respects its
structure and decorations are tasteless: for it demonstrates to us
the presence of people who are cultivated at least from *one* point

of view. How doubly agreeable it is for us, therefore, when the spirit of a higher culture, even if only a sensuous one, greets us from a human habitation.

This became very vividly clear to me at my uncle's castle. I had heard and read a great deal about art; Philo himself was a great picture lover and had a fine collection; I too had done a lot of sketching; but on the other hand I had been too concerned with my own feelings and aimed only at putting in order in the first place the one thing that is needed, on the other hand all that I had seen seemed to be a distraction to me, like the rest of the worldly things. Now for the first time I had been led back to myself by something external, and I learnt now to appreciate to my great astonishment the difference between the excellent natural song of the nightingale and a four-part hallelujah from sensitive human throats.

I did not hide my happiness at this new insight from my uncle who was in the habit of conversing in particular with me when all the others had gone to take up their activities. He spoke about what he possessed and had produced with great modesty, and with great assurance about the intention in which it had been collected and set up, and I could in fact perceive that he was speaking with consideration for me when in his old way he seemed to be subordinating the good, of which he believed himself to be the lord and master, to what according to my conviction was the true and the best.

'If we can think it possible,' he once said, 'that the Creator of the world Himself assumed the shape of His own creature and remained on earth for a time in this fashion, this creature must already seem to us to be infinitely perfect, because the Creator could be so intimately united with him. There can, therefore, be no contradiction between the concept of man and that of the divinity, and even if we do often feel a certain dissimilarity and remoteness from the divinity, it is all the more our duty not always to be looking only at the infirmities and weaknesses of our nature, like the advocate of the evil one, but rather to search out all the perfections by means of which we can confirm the claims of our similarity to God.'

I smiled and rejoined: 'Don't put me too much to shame, dear Uncle, by your kindness in speaking in my language! What you have to say to me is of so great importance for me that I should like to hear it in your most personal language, and I will then attempt to translate any parts of it that I cannot wholly appropriate.'

'I shall be able to continue in my very own way as well, without any change of tone', he then said. 'It probably remains man's greatest merit when he can determine circumstances as much as possible and can let himself be determined as little as possible by them. The whole universe lies before us, like a great quarry before the master-builder, who only deserves this name if he can put together with the greatest economy, purposiveness and firmness these chance natural masses according to a primal image formed in his own mind. Everything apart from ourselves consists only of elements, indeed I may well say everything about us; but there lies deep within us this creative force which is able to call into being what is to be and does not let us pause or rest until we have given expression to it outside ourselves or about ourselves, in one way or another. You, dear niece, have perhaps chosen the better part; you have sought to bring your moral being and your profound, lovable nature into harmony with yourself and with the highest Being, whereas we others are also not to be blamed, I believe, when we try to get to know the range of sensuous man and bring him actively to unity.'

We gradually became closer as a result of such conversations, and I obtained from him that he talked with me as with himself, without indulgence. 'Don't think that I am flattering you,' the Uncle said, 'when I praise your way of thinking and acting. I respect a person who knows clearly what he wants, who goes onwards unceasingly, who is familiar with the means to his end and who knows how to take hold of these means and to use them; how far his purpose may be great or trivial, may deserve praise or blame, is something that I do not take into account until later. Believe me, my dear, the greatest part of the disasters and of what is called evil in the world arises merely because people are too negligent to know their own purposes properly, and if they do know such aims, to work seriously towards their realization. They seem to me to be like people who have the idea that a tower can and must be built and yet do not use more stones and labour on the foundations than would be intercepted from building a cottage. If you, my friend, whose highest need has been to come to an understanding with your own inward moral nature, had simply contented yourself between your family, a fiancé and perhaps a husband instead of making great and bold sacrifices, you would never have enjoyed a contented moment and would have been eternally at odds with yourself.'

'You use the word sacrifice,' I put in here, 'and I have often thought how we bring something of lesser value as an offering to a higher purpose, as if to a divinity, although it is clear to us, just as we would gladly and willingly bring a beloved sheep to the sacrificial altar for the sake of the health of an honoured father.'

'Whatever it may be,' he rejoined, 'reason or emotion, that tells us to give one thing for another, or one thing in preference to another, decisiveness and consistency are in my opinion the most admirable qualities about man. You can't have the goods and the money at the same time; and the man who always longs for the goods without having the heart to hand over the money is in just as bad a position as the man who regrets the transaction when he has the goods in his hands. But I am far from blaming people for this reason; for it is not they who are really guilty, but the complex situation in which they find themselves and in which they are not able to control themselves. Thus for example you will find on the average fewer bad managers in the country than in the towns, and again fewer in small towns than in large ones; and why is this? Man is born to fit into a limited situation; he can understand simple, close and definite purposes, and he gets used to employing the means which are near at hand; but as soon as he goes any distance, he knows neither what he will nor what he should be doing, and it is all one whether he is distracted by the large number of the objects or whether he is put out by their greatness and dignity. It is always a misfortune when a man is induced to strive for something with which he cannot associate himself through some regular spontaneous activity.

'Indeed,' he continued, 'nothing is possible in the world without seriousness, and in fact there is little seriousness to be found among those whom we call cultured people; they approach work, business and the arts, and even pleasures, only with a kind of defensiveness, as I see it; these people live in the way one reads a heap of newspapers, only in order to get rid of them, and this reminds me of that young Englishman in Rome who one evening at a social gathering reported in a very satisfied way that on that day he had done six churches and two art-galleries. We like to know about and be familiar with all sorts of things, in particular what concerns us least, we do not notice that no hunger is assuaged when we snatch at air. When I first meet someone, I at once ask what he occupies himself with, and how, and in what sequence, and with the answering of these questions my interest in him is also determined on a lifetime basis.'

'Perhaps, dear Uncle,' I added, 'you are too strict and withdraw your helping hand from some good people to whom you could be useful.'

'Is he to be blamed,' he answered, 'who has worked at them and about them for so long in vain? How much do we not suffer in our youth from people who believe they are inviting us to a pleasant

party when they promise to bring us into the company of the
Danaides or Sisyphus. Thank God, I have separated myself from
them, and if one of these people unfortunately comes into my
circle, I try to bow him out in the most polite way possible: for it is
precisely from these people that we hear the bitterest complaints
about the confused course of world affairs, about the shallowness
of science, about the frivolity of artists, about the emptiness of
poets, and I don't know what else. It is they who think least that
they themselves and the crowd, who are like them, would not read
the very book which would be written according to their
requirements, that genuine literature is alien to them, and that
even a good work of art could only obtain their approval because
of prejudice. But let us break off, this is no time for scolding or
complaining.'

He directed my attention to the various pictures which were on
the wall; my eye was caught by those whose aspect was attractive
or whose subject was significant; he let this happen for a time, and
then he said: 'Do now pay some attention also to the skilful spirit
that brought forth these works. Good minds like so much to see
the hand of God in nature; why should we not also give some
consideration to the hand of His imitator?' He then drew my
attention to pictures that were not of an arresting quality, and
tried to explain to me that in fact only the history of art could give
us understanding of the value and dignity of a work of art, and
that in the first place we must know about the difficult stages of
mechanism and craft, by means of which gifted men have been
working themselves upward over the centuries, if we are to
understand how it is possible that the genius can move freely and
cheerfully on the high peak, the sight of which alone causes us
giddiness.

With this in mind he had brought together a beautiful
collection of works, and as he interpreted them to me, I could not
help seeing before me here a symbolic representation of moral
development. When I told him what I was thinking, he went on:
'You are completely right, and we can see from this that it is not
good to give oneself up to moral development if one remains alone
and wrapped up in oneself; we shall find rather that he whose
spirit aspires to moral cultivation has every reason to develop a
refinement of the senses at the same time, in order that he shan't
get into danger of slipping down from his moral heights by
yielding to the allurements of an unguarded imagination and by
getting into a position where he demeans his higher nature by
taking pleasure in tasteless fripperies, if not in something worse.'

I did not suspect him of alluding to myself, but I took what he said to heart, when I recalled that among the hymns that had helped me there were a number that may well have been insipid, and that the little pictures which had been linked with my spiritual ideas would hardly have found favour in my uncle's eyes.

In the meantime Philo had often spent time in the library and he now introduced me to it. We admired the selection and also the number of the books. They were in every sense a considered collection: for almost only those books were to be found there which lead us to clear perception or direct us to right order, which either provide us with the right materials or convince us of the unity of our intellect.

In the course of my life I had read very much, and in some subjects there was hardly a book that I did not know; it was, therefore, all the more pleasant to speak here of a prospect of the whole and to notice gaps, whereas elsewhere I had only seen limited confusion or unending extension.

At this time we made the acquaintance of a very interesting, quiet man. He was a doctor and naturalist, and seemed to belong more to the Penates than to the dwellers in the house. He showed us the natural history collection which like the library was in enclosed glass cases, and both decorated the walls of the rooms and ennobled the space without confining it. Here I was happily reminded of my childhood, and showed my father several objects which he had in the past brought to the sickbed of his child when she was hardly looking out at the world. On this occasion the doctor concealed as little as in subsequent discussions the fact that he was approaching me with religious views in mind; in so doing he praised the Uncle highly on account of his tolerance and his respect for everything that demonstrated and encouraged the value and unity of human personality; it was true, however, that he did demand a similar approach from all other people, he said, and that there was nothing that he did not habitually condemn or shun as much as individual self-conceit and a narrowness that was excluding in effect.

After my sister's wedding ceremony the Uncle's eyes shone with joy, and he talked to me on various occasions about what he was thinking of doing for her and her children. He had fine estates which he managed himself and which he was hoping to pass on to his nephews in the best condition. He seemed to cherish particular thoughts with regard to the small estate on which we were at the time: 'I shall leave it only to someone who is able to know, value and enjoy what it contains,' he said, 'and who appreciates how much a rich man of rank, especially in Germany, has reason to establish something exemplary.'

By this time most of the guests had gradually disappeared; we prepared to take our leave and believed that we had experienced the last festive scene, when we were once more surprised by his attentiveness in wishing to present us with an entertainment of good quality. We had not been able to conceal from him the delight which we had felt when an unaccompanied choir sang at my sister's wedding. We suggested to him that he might provide us with a repetition of that pleasure; he did not seem to pay attention. Therefore how surprised we were when he said to us one evening: 'The dance music has finished; our young and fleeting friends have left us, the married couple themselves already look more serious than they did a few days ago, and parting from one another at such a time, when we shall perhaps never see each other again, or if we do see each other again, shall see each other differently, stirs within us a solemn mood which I cannot encourage in a nobler manner than by means of a type of music whose repetition you had seemed to wish for earlier.'

He arranged for the choir, which in the meantime had been reinforced and had yet more practice in private, to present to us songs in four-part and eight-part harmony which really, I may well say, gave us a foretaste of heavenly bliss. Up to now I had only known the pious singing with which good souls often believe that they are praising God with hoarse throats like the little birds in the woods, because they are giving themselves a pleasant feeling; and then the conceited music of concerts in which we are at all events carried away to the admiration of talent, but rarely even only to a transient pleasure. I now heard music which had originated from the deepest imagination of the finest characters and which by means of particular and practised voices in harmonic unity again spoke to man's most profound and outstanding faculty and caused him really to feel vividly at this moment his likeness to God. They were all ecclesiastical songs in Latin, displayed like jewels in the golden ring of well-mannered secular society and raising me up to spiritual heights and giving me happiness without any demand for so-called devotional edification.

At our departure we all received most generous presents. He presented me with the cross of the order of my foundation, worked and enamelled more artistically and more beautifully than such could usually be seen. It hung from a large brilliant, by means of which it was fastened on to the ribbon at the same time; he asked me to see it as the noblest stone in a natural history collection.

My sister now went with her husband to his estates, while the rest of us went back to our dwelling-places and, as far as our outer circumstances were concerned, we seemed to have come back to a wholly commonplace life. We had come down to earth, as if from a fairy castle, and again had to act and make do in our usual manner.

The special experiences which I had in that new circle left me with a beautiful impression; but it did not remain long in its complete vividness, although the Uncle tried to maintain and renew it by sending me from time to time some of his best and most pleasing works of art and by exchanging them again for others, when I had been enjoying them a sufficiently long time.

I was too accustomed to being concerned with myself, to putting the affairs of my heart and spirit in order and to conversing about them with like-minded people for me to be able to study a work of art attentively without soon returning to myself. I was used only to looking at paintings or engravings as if they were the letters of a book. Pleasant printing is completely agreeable; but who will take a book in his hand for the sake of the printing? Similarly a pictorial representation should say something to me, should instruct, move and improve me; and the Uncle could say what he liked in the letters with which he commented on his works of art, I continued in my old way.

However, it was outward events, the changes in my family situation more than my own personality, that deflected me from such considerations, indeed for a time from myself; I had to be patient and to be active, to a greater degree than seemed possible to my weak powers.

My unmarried sister had been my right arm hitherto; healthy, strong and inexpressibly good-natured, she had taken on the oversight of the household as the personal care for our old father occupied me. She was overcome by catarrh that developed into consumption, and in three weeks she was lying on her bier; her death struck me with wounds whose scars I still do not care to look at.

I lay ill in bed before she had yet been buried; the old trouble on my chest seemed to flare up again, I coughed violently and was so hoarse that I could scarcely bring forth any loud sound.

My married sister came into premature labour as a result of the shock and grief. My old father was afraid of losing both his children and his hope of descendants; his justified tears increased my misery; I prayed to God for my restoration to tolerable health and begged Him only to allow me to live until after Father's death. I recovered and was well, in my own way.

My sister became pregnant again. Various cares, which in such cases are confided to the mother, were shared with me; she was not entirely happy with her husband, and that was to be kept secret from Father: I had to be arbitrator and was able to take on this role all the more easily as my brother-in-law had confidence in me and both were really good people, except that both of them, instead of being indulgent to one another, remonstrated with each other and could never be truly at one because of their desire to be living in complete unity together. Now I was learning to take up worldly problems in earnest as well and to practice what previously I had only sung about.

My sister gave birth to a son; my father's indisposition did not prevent him travelling to her. He was unbelievably bright and cheerful at seeing the child, and during the christening ceremony he seemed to me to be in a state of rapture contrary to his usual manner, indeed, I might say he appeared as a guardian angel with two faces. With the one he was looking happily forward into those regions which he hoped to enter soon, and with the other he was looking at the new, hopeful, earthly life which had come into being in the baby boy that was descended from him. On the return journey he did not tire of talking to me about the child, about his build, his health and the wish that the innate tendencies of this new citizen of the world might be happily developed. His observations in this context continued when we arrived home, and it was not until a few days later that a kind of fever became noticeable which showed itself after he had dined in a somewhat exhausting heat, but without any shivering.

He did not take to his bed, however, went out in the mornings and carried on conscientiously with his adminstrative duties until finally he was prevented from doing so by continuing serious symptoms.

I shall never forget the quietness of mind, the clarity and distinctness with which he undertook in most orderly fashion to deal with the affairs of his household and to arrange for his own burial, as if it were someone else's concern.

With a cheerfulness which was not otherwise characteristic of him and which became heightened to vivacious joy, he said to me: 'Where has the fear of death gone which I certainly used to feel? Ought I to be reluctant to die? I have a merciful God, the grave arouses no terrors within me, I have an eternal life.'

To recall the circumstances of his death, which occurred soon afterwards, is one of my pleasantest occupations in my solitude, and nobody will persuade me that the visible effects of a higher power were not at work here.

The death of my dear father changed my way of life as it had been up to then. I moved from strict obedience and severe

limitation to great freedom, and I enjoyed it like a food which one
has been without for a long time. Previously I had seldom been
out of the house for two hours; now I scarcely spent a day in my
room. My friends, to whom earlier I had only been able to pay
hasty visits, wished to enjoy my continuing presence, just as I did
theirs; I was frequently asked out to dine, drives by carriage and
little pleasure-trips were added, and I nowhere held back. But
when the circle of activities had been passed through, I realized
that the inestimable happiness of freedom does not consist in our
doing everything which we like doing and to which circumstances
invite us, but in our being able to do what we think right and
proper without hindrance or reservation and by the straight path,
and I was old enough in this instance to arrive at this fine
conviction without having to pay for the experience.

What I could not deny myself was to continue and take up more
closely, as soon as might be possible, my association with the
members of the Moravian community, and I hastened to attend
one of their next meetings: but even there I by no means found
what I had expected. I was honest enough to let my opinion be
noticed, and in return the attempt was made to teach me that this
gathering was nothing in comparison with a properly organized
community. I could not accept this; for according to my
conviction the true spirit should be visible in a small meeting as
well as in a large organization.

One of their bishops who was present, a direct pupil of the
Count, busied himself a lot with me; he spoke perfect English, and
as I understand it a little, he thought that this was a hint that we
belonged together; but I did not think so at all; association with
him could give me not the slightest pleasure. He was a cutler and
a native of Moravia; his way of thinking could not help showing
an artisan-like quality. I got on better with Herr von L., who had
been a major in French service; but I never felt capable of the
subservience which he showed to his superiors; indeed, I felt as if I
were being given a box on the ear when I saw the major's wife and
other more or less esteemed ladies kiss the bishop's hand. None the
less a journey to Holland was planned, though it never
materialized, which was certainly for the best, as far as I was
concerned.

My sister had given birth to a daughter, and now it was the
turn of us women to be pleased and to think how at some future
time she should be educated like ourselves. My brother-in-law, on
the other hand, was very discontented when a further daughter
followed in the next year; with his large estates, he wished to see
boys around him who would be able to assist him in the
administration in the future.

Because of my weak health I kept quiet and maintained a fairly equal balance with a tranquil way of life; I was not afraid of death, in fact I wished to die, but I felt in the stillness that God was giving me time to examine my soul and to come ever more closely to him. During the many sleepless nights I felt in particular something that I cannot really describe precisely.

It was as if my soul were able to think without the presence of the body; it regarded the body itself as an alien entity, rather as one looks upon a dress. It recollected past times and events with an extraordinary vivacity, and sensed from these what would ensue. All these times are past; what is to come will also pass on: the body will be torn to pieces like a dress, but I, the familiar I, I am.

I was taught to give myself up as little as I possibly could to this great, exalted and comforting feeling by a noble friend who linked himself ever more closely to me; this was the doctor whom I had met at my uncle's house and who had become very well informed concerning the state of my body and my mind; he showed me how much these emotions, if we nourish them within ourselves independently of outward objects, hollow us out, as it were, and undermine the ground of our existence. 'Man's first designation is to be active,' he said, 'and he should make use of all intervening periods in which he has been compelled to rest to acquire a clear perception of outward things, and this will again make activity in the future easier for him.'

As my friend knew about my habit of regarding my own body as an outward object, and as he knew that I was pretty familiar with my constitution, my malady and the medicinal resources, and that I had really become half a doctor because of my own and other people's continuing sufferings, he directed my attention away from the knowledge of the human body and medicaments to the other, neighbouring objects of creation, leading me about as if in the Garden of Eden, and only at the end, if I may continue my analogy, did he allow me to have a distant presentiment of the Creator walking in the Garden in the cool of evening.

How glad I was now to see God in nature, since I bore Him with such certainty in my heart; how interesting to me was the work of His hands, and how grateful I was that He had been willing to give me life with the breath of His mouth!

We hoped anew, with my sister, for the birth of a baby boy; my brother-in-law looked forward longingly to him, but he unfortunately did not live to see his birth. The worthy man died from the after-effects of an unfortunate fall from a horse, and my sister followed him after she had given birth to a lovely boy. It was only with sadness that I could look at her four orphaned children. So many healthy persons had passed on before myself, the invalid; was I not perhaps destined to see some of these hopeful blossoms fall? I knew the world well enough to be aware amid how many dangers a child grows up, particularly in the upper classes, and it seemed to me as if these dangers had increased even further for present-day society since the time of my youth. I felt that I in my weak state of health was in no position to do much, or anything, for the children; all the more welcome to me, therefore, was the Uncle's decision, which arose naturally from his way of thinking, to direct his whole attention to the upbringing of these charming children. And certainly, they deserved it in every sense, they were well-formed and all promised to become good-natured and intelligent people, for all the great differences between them.

After my good doctor had brought the matter to my attention, I liked to observe family resemblances in children and relatives. My father had carefully preserved the pictures of his forbears and had portraits of himself and his children painted by tolerably good artists; my mother and her relations had not been forgotten either. We knew the characteristics of the whole family precisely and as we had often compared them together, we now looked out for similarities of external and internal nature. My sister's eldest son seemed to resemble his paternal grandfather, of whom a very well painted youthful picture had been included in our uncle's collection; he too, like his grandfather, who had always shown himself as a worthy officer, loved nothing more than firearms, with which he occupied himself whenever he visited me. For my father had left a very fine firearms cabinet, and the little boy would not be content until I presented him with a brace of pistols and a shotgun, and until he had found out how to handle a German lock. On the other hand he was anything but rough in his actions and his whole character, in fact rather gentle and cautious.

The eldest daughter had captivated my liking completely, and this may have been because she looked like me and because she kept most closely to me of all four. But I may well say that the more closely I observed her as she grew up, the more she put me to shame, and I could not look at the child without admiration, indeed I may almost say, not without respect. It would not be easy to find a nobler figure nor a calmer disposition, nor someone whose activity, like hers, was always steady and not confined to one object. At no moment of her life was she without occupation, and every undertaking became a worthwhile activity in her hands. Everything seemed of equal importance to her, so long only as she could carry out what was appropriate at the time and place, and likewise she could remain quiet and without impatience when there was nothing to be done. At no other time in my life have I seen activity of this kind, without the requirement of an occupation. From childhood onwards her behaviour towards those who were suffering and in need of help was matchless. I gladly admit that I never had the ability to make a business out of philanthropy; I was not mean to the poor, indeed I often gave too much to them in relation to my circumstances, but to a certain extent I was only buying myself off, and someone had to be linked to me by birth if he wanted to acquire attention from me. I can commend exactly the opposite in my niece's case. I have never seen her give a poor person money, and what she received from me for this purpose she always first converted into the objects immediately required. To me she never seemed more delightful than when she was plundering my wardrobes and linen-cupboards; she always found something that I did not wear and did not need, and it gave her the greatest happiness to cut these old things up and to make them suitable for some ragged child.

The attitudes of her sister were already showing themselves to be different; she had much of her mother about her, gave promise early on of becoming very dainty and attractive, and she seems to be trying to keep her promise; she is much concerned with her outward appearance and from early days onward she has known how to dress up and comport herself in a very striking way. I still remember with what rapture she looked at herself in the mirror as a child when I fastened round her neck for her the beautiful pearls which my mother had bequeathed to her and which she discovered by chance with me.

Whenever I considered these various inclinations, it was agreeable for me to imagine how my possessions after my death would be divided among them and come to life again through them. I saw my father's shotguns again moving around the open country on my nephew's back and birds again tumbling out of his game-bag; I saw my entire wardrobe coming out of church at the Easter confirmation service, having been adapted to the needs of none but little girls, and a modest middle-class girl adorned on her wedding-day with my best materials: for Natalie had a particular liking for the provision of such children and respectable poor girls, although, as I must note here, she gave no sign at all of any need of dependence on a visible person or an invisible Being, such as had shown itself in so lively a manner in my own case when I was young.

When I then thought that on the very same day the youngest girl would be taking my pearls and jewels to wear at court, I could be calm at the prospect of my possessions, like my body, being given back to the elements.

The children have been growing apace, and I am happy to say that they are healthy, lovely and brave creatures. I put up patiently with the fact that the Uncle keeps them away from me at a distance, and I seldom see them when they are in the neighbourhood or indeed in the city.

The supervision of all the children, who are educated at different places and are lodged now here, now there, is in the hands of a strange man who is taken to be a French clergyman, but without there being any real information about his origins.

At first I could see no plan in this education, until my doctor finally revealed to me that the Uncle had let himself be convinced by the Abbé that if one wished to do something about a person's education, one would need to see in which directions his inclinations and wishes would move. Then one would have to put him in a position where he could satisfy his inclinations and fulfil his wishes as soon as possible, so that if he should have made a mistake, he should be aware of his error in good time, and if he had found what suited him, he should hold to it the more keenly and continue his training it all the more industriously. My wish is that this strange experiment may succeed; with children of such good temperament it is perhaps possible.

But what I cannot approve in these pedagogues is that they attempt to remove from the children anything that might lead them to intimate association with themselves and with the invisible, only faithful Friend. Indeed, it often annoys me about the Uncle that he thinks me to be a danger to the children on this account. In practice nobody is really tolerant! For he who asserts that he is glad to let everyone have his own manner and character, none the less always tries to exclude from an activity those who do not think as he does.

This way of keeping the children from me distresses me all the more, the more convinced I become of the reality of my faith. Why should it not have a divine origin and a real object, since it shows itself to be so effective in practical life? If it is practical experience that makes us for the first time really aware of our own being, why should we not be able to convince ourselves by the same way of that Being Who extends His hand to us for everything that is good?

The facts that I always go forward, and never back, that my actions come ever more to resemble the idea of perfection that I have set up for myself, and that every day I feel it easier to do what I think right, even with the weak state of my body, that denies me so many a service; can all these things be explained from human nature into whose corruption I have had so much insight? Not for me, certainly.

I can scarcely remember a commandment; nothing appears to me in the shape of a law; it is an instinct that leads me and always guides me aright; I follow my opinions in freedom and know as little about restriction as about remorse. Thank God that I recognize to Whom I owe this happiness, and that I may only think of these excellences with humility. For I shall never run into the danger of being proud of my own ability and power, since I have recognized so clearly what a monster may be produced and nurtured in every human breast, unless a higher Power preserves us.

Select Bibliography

Here are a few references for further reading; in most cases these works include bibliographical information:

GOETHE, 'Weimarer' or 'Sophienausgabe', 143 vols., 1887-1920 (*Wilhelm Meisters Lehrjahre* in vols. 21-23); 'Hamburger Ausgabe', 21 vols., 1948-69 (*Lehrjahre* in vol. 7); 'Gedenkausgabe', 27 vols., 1948-71 (*Lehrjahre* in vol. 7). [Erich Trunz's notes in vol. 7 of the 'Hamburger Ausgabe' have been gratefully used; the footnotes in the text that follows derive mainly from this source.]

BLACKALL, E. A., *Goethe and the Novel* (1976)

BRUFORD, W. H., *Theatre, drama and audience in Goethe's Germany* (1950)

BRUFORD, W. H., *Culture and society in Classical Weimar, 1775-1805* (1962)

FAIRLEY, B., *A study of Goethe* (1947)

GRAY, R., *Goethe: A critical introduction* (1967)

KORFF, H. A. *Geist der Goethezeit* (1923-41)

MÜLLER, G., *Kleine Goethe-Bibliographie* (1947)

PASCAL, R., *The German novel* (1956)

REISS, H., *Goethe's novels* (1969)

STAIGER, E., *Goethe* (1952-59)

VIETOR, K., *Goethe* (1948)

Principal Dates of Goethe's Life

1749	Born at Frankfurt am Main
1765	Studied at Leipzig
1770-71	Studied law at Strassburg
1772	Spent some months in Wetzlar at the supreme court of the Empire
1773	*Götz von Berlichingen* (prose drama)
1774	*Clavigo* (prose drama)
1774	*Die Leiden des jungen Werthers* (novel)
1775	Becomes companion to the young Duke Karl August at Weimar and subsequently becomes much involved in administrative work there.
1786-88	Journey to Italy
1787	*Iphigenie auf Tauris* (verse drama)
1788	*Egmont* (prose drama)
1788	After returning to Weimar from Italy, beginning of relationship with Christiane Vulpius.
1789	*Torquato Tasso* (verse drama)
	Birth of August, son of Goethe and Christiane.
1790	*Faust. Ein Fragment* (verse drama)
1791	Becomes artistic director of the Weimar court theatre, remaining in this office until 1817.
1792-93	Accompanies the Duke Karl August on campaign against France.
1795	*Unterhaltungen deutscher Ausgewanderten* (prose fiction)
1795	*Römische Elegien* (cycle of poems)
1795-96	*Wilhelm Meisters Lehrjahre* (novel)
1797	*Hermann und Dorothea* (verse epic)
1803	*Die natürliche Tochter* (verse drama)
1806	Marriage to Christiane
1808	*Faust. Erster Teil* (verse drama)
1809	*Die Wahlverwandtschaften* (novel)
1809	*Pandora* (masque in verse)
1811-33	*Dichtung und Wahrheit* (autobiography)
1816	Death of Christiane
1816-17	*Italienische Reise* (autobiography)
1819	*West-östlicher Divan* (cycle of poems)
1828	*Novelle* (prose fiction)
1829	*Wilhelm Meisters Wanderjahre* (final version of the second part of the novel)

PRINCIPAL DATES OF GOETHE'S LIFE

| 1832 | Death of Goethe |
| 1833 | *Faust. Der Tragödie zweiter Teil* (verse drama) |